SEASONS OF LOVE

CROCHETED SWEATERS FOR THE FAMILY

BY MELISSA LEAPMAN

LEISURE ARTS, INC.
Little Rock, Arkansas

SEASONS OF LOVE
CROCHETED SWEATERS FOR THE FAMILY

BY MELISSA LEAPMAN

EDITORIAL STAFF

Vice President and Editor-at-Large:
Anne Van Wagner Childs
Vice President and Editor-in-Chief:
Sandra Graham Case
Director of Designer Relations:
Debra Nettles
Editorial Director: Susan Frantz Wiles
Publications Director:
Susan White Sullivan
Creative Art Director: Gloria Bearden
Photography Director: Karen Hall
Art Operations Director: Jeff Curtis

PRODUCTION
Managing Editor: Valesha M. Kirksey
Senior Technical Editor: Linda Luder
Instructional Editor: Sarah J. Green

EDITORIAL
Managing Editor: Suzie Puckett

ART
Senior Art Director: Rhonda Shelby
Senior Production Artist: Lora Puls
Production Artists: Catherine Harris,
Dana Vaughn, and Wendy Willets
Color Technician: Mark Hawkins
Photography Stylists: Sondra Daniel,
Tiffany Huffman, and Janna Laughlin
Contributing Photographer: Ken West of
Peerless Photography
Publishing Systems Administrator:
Becky Riddle
Publishing Systems Assistants:
Myra S. Means and
Chris Wertenberger

BUSINESS STAFF

Publisher: Rick Barton
Vice President, Finance:
Tom Siebenmorgen
**Director of Corporate Planning and
Development:** Laticia Mull Cornett
Vice President, Retail Marketing:
Bob Humphrey
Vice President, Sales: Ray Shelgosh
Vice President, National Accounts:
Pam Stebbins
Director of Sales and Service:
Margaret Sweetin
Retail Customer Service Manager:
Wanda Price
Vice President, Operations: Jim Dittrich
Comptroller, Operations: Rob Thieme
Print Production Manager: Fred F. Pruss

Softcover ISBN 1-57486-247-2

To Michael with much love

Acknowledgments

I would like to thank the following talented individuals for working on the samples photographed in this book: Denise Augostine, James G. Davis, Marianne Forrestal, Carole Minchew, JoAnn Moss, Barbara Pretzsch, Sharon Ryman, MarriAnn Schweitzer, and Kim Wiltfang.

I'm grateful to the yarn and button companies who generously supplied materials for these sweaters. Their beautiful products have provided me with tremendous inspiration and pleasure throughout my design career.

Special thanks go to Debra Nettles at Leisure Arts, Inc. for helping to create this wonderful opportunity and for her many years of encouragement and support.

Finally, to Ann E. Smith, my peerless pattern editor, many thanks and much love.

Contents

Introduction

I always get excited about presenting a handmade gift to someone special. It is much more than simply a way of showing off my crochet skills. It is a way of sharing a part of myself!

For this book, I have designed a new collection of 24 fun-to-make and easy-to-give sweaters. There's something for everyone, including Mom, Dad, and kids of all ages— even babies. You'll find projects for every season and occasion, from a delicate summer cardigan to a Nordic-inspired pullover. And they use all of my favorite, widely available yarns!

It was fun creating these patterns for you. I hope you enjoy making and sharing the finished sweaters with your family and friends. After all, when you crochet from your heart, you are giving wonderful, heart-warming gifts to your loved ones!

— *Melissa Leapman*

winter white trio

Translate a favorite knitted classic into crochet with this cozy threesome. Post stitches and popcorns create the beautiful texture.

Man's Honeycomb Pullover

INTERMEDIATE SKILL LEVEL

SIZES

Man's Small (Medium, Large, Extra-Large). Instructions are for smallest size, with changes for other sizes noted in parentheses as necessary.

FINISHED MEASUREMENTS

Chest: 42 (47½, 53, 59)"
Length: 26 (27, 27½, 28½)"
Sleeve width at underarm: 19 (20, 21, 22)"

MATERIALS

Lion Brand's *Wool-Ease* (worsted weight; 80% acrylic/20% wool; 3 oz; approx 197 yds), 11 (12, 13, 13) skeins Fisherman #099
Crochet hooks, sizes G/6 and H/8 or size needed to obtain gauge

GAUGE

With larger hook, in Honeycomb Patt, 14 sts and 11 rows = 4".
To measure your gauge, make a test swatch as follows: With larger hook, ch 24. Hdc into third ch from hook and into each ch across. Ch 2, turn. Work Honeycomb Patt for ten rows. Fasten off.
Piece should measure 6½" wide and 4" long. **To save time, take time to check gauge.**

NOTES

To decrease, work a dec hdc to combine the first 2 sts and/or the last 2 sts of the row.
Dec hdc = (Yarn over, insert hook into next st and pull up a loop) twice, yarn over and draw it through all five loops on hook.

To increase, work 2 sts into one st. Each hdc, FPDC, BPDC, FPTR, FPDTR, turning-ch-3 and turning-ch-2 counts as one st.
FPTR and FPDTR are referred to as FPSTS.

RIB PATT

(Over an odd number of ch)
Foundation Row (RS): Dc into fourth ch from hook and into each ch across. Ch 2, turn.
Row 1 (WS): Skip first st, *FPDC into next st, BPDC into next st. Repeat from * across, ending row with FPDC into next st, hdc into top of turning-ch. Ch 2, turn.
Row 2: Skip first st, *BPDC into next st, FPDC into next st. Repeat from * across, ending row with BPDC into next st, hdc into top of turning-ch-2. Ch 2, turn.
Repeat Rows 1 and 2 for patt.

HONEYCOMB PATT

(Mult. 10 + 3 sts)
Foundation Row (WS): Skip first st, hdc into each st across, ending row with hdc into top of turning-ch-2. Ch 2, turn.
Row 1 (RS): Skip first st, hdc into next st, *FPTR into next 2 sts two rows below, skip the 2 hdc behind the 2 FPSTS just made, hdc into next 5 hdc, FPTR into next 2 sts two rows below, skip the 2 hdc behind the 2 FPSTS just made, hdc into next st. Repeat from * across, ending row with hdc into top of turning-ch. Ch 2, turn.
Row 2 and all WS rows: Skip first st, hdc into each st across, ending row with hdc into top of turning-ch-2. Ch 2, turn.

Row 3: Skip first st, hdc into next 3 sts, *FPDTR into 2 FPSTS two rows below, skip the 2 hdc behind the 2 FPSTS just made, hdc into next hdc, FPDTR into next 2 FPSTS two rows below, skip the 2 hdc behind the 2 FPSTS just made, hdc into next 5 hdc. Repeat from * across, ending row with FPDTR into 2 FPSTS two rows below, skip 2 hdc behind the 2 FPSTS just made, hdc into next hdc, FPDTR into next 2 FPSTS two rows below, skip the 2 hdc behind the 2 FPSTS just made, hdc into next 3 hdc, hdc into top of turning-ch-2. Ch 2, turn.
Row 5: Skip first st, hdc into next 3 hdc, *FPTR into next 2 FPSTS two rows below, skip the 2 hdc behind the 2 FPSTS just made, hdc into next hdc, FPTR into next 2 FPSTS two rows below, skip the 2 hdc behind the 2 FPSTS just made, hdc into next 5 hdc. Repeat from * across, ending row with FPTR into next 2 FPSTS two rows below, skip the 2 hdc behind the 2 FPSTS just made, hdc into next hdc, FPTR into next 2 FPSTS two rows below, skip the 2 hdc behind the 2 FPSTS just made, hdc into next 3 hdc, hdc into top of turning-ch-2. Ch 2, turn.
Row 7: Skip first st, hdc into next hdc, *FPDTR into next 2 FPSTS two rows below, skip the 2 hdc behind the 2 FPSTS just made, hdc into next 5 hdc, FPDTR into next 2 FPSTS two rows below, skip the 2 hdc behind the 2 FPSTS just made, hdc into next hdc. Repeat from * across, ending row with hdc into top of turning-ch-2. Ch 2, turn.
Row 8: As Row 2.
Repeat Rows 1-8 for patt.

BACK

With smaller hook, ch 75 (85, 95, 105). Work Rib Patt until piece measures approx 2¹/₂" from beg, ending after WS row—73 (83, 93, 103) sts each row. Change to larger hook, ch 2, turn.

Next Row (RS): Hdc into each st across, ending row with hdc into top of turning-ch-2—73 (83, 93, 103) sts. Ch 2, turn.

Next Row: Work Foundation Row of Honeycomb Patt—73 (83, 93, 103) sts.

Cont even in Honeycomb Patt until piece measures approx 25¹/₂ (26¹/₂, 27, 28)" from beg, ending after WS row. Ch 2, turn.

Shape Neck: Next Row (RS): Cont in Honeycomb Patt as established, and work across first 22 (27, 32, 37) sts, ch 2, turn, leaving rest of row unworked. Cont even on this side until piece measures 26 (27, 27¹/₂, 28¹/₂)" from beg. Fasten off.

For second side of neck, with RS facing, skip the middle 29 sts, attach yarn with a slip st to next st and ch 2. Complete as for first side.

FRONT

Work as for back until piece measures approx 23 (24, 24¹/₂, 25¹/₂)" from beg, ending after WS row. Ch 2, turn.

Shape Neck: Next Row (RS): Cont in Honeycomb Patt as established, and work across first 28 (33, 38, 43) sts, ch 2, turn, leaving rest of row unworked. Dec 1 st at neck edge every row five times, then every other row

once—22 (27, 32, 37) sts rem. Cont even on this side until it measures same as back to shoulders. Fasten off.

For second side of neck, with RS facing, skip the middle 17 sts and attach yarn with a slip st to next st and ch 2. Complete as for first side.

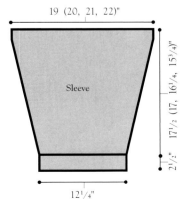

SLEEVES

With smaller hook, ch 45. Work Rib Patt until piece measures approx 2¹/₂" from beg, ending after RS row—43 sts each row. Change to larger hook, ch 2, turn.

Next Row (WS): Work Foundation Row of Honeycomb Patt—43 sts.

Cont in Honeycomb Patt as established, and inc 1 st each side every other row 2 (6, 9, 14) times, then every fourth row 10 (8, 6, 3) times—67 (71, 73, 77) sts—working new sts into Honeycomb Patt. Cont even until sleeve measures approx 20 (19¹/₂, 18³/₄, 18¹/₄)" from beg. Fasten off.

FINISHING

Sew shoulder seams.

Neckband: With RS facing and smaller hook, attach yarn with a slip st to neck edge of left shoulder seam and ch 3.

Rnd 1: Work 75 dc evenly around neckline. Join with a slip st to top of ch-3. Ch 2, do not turn.

Rnd 2: Skip first st, *FPDC into next st, BPDC into next st. Repeat from * around, ending rnd with FPDC, slip st to top of ch-2. Ch 2.

Repeat last rnd until band measures approx 1" from beg. Fasten off.

Place markers 9¹/₂ (10, 10¹/₂, 11)" down from shoulders. Set in sleeves between markers. Sew sleeve and side seams.

8¹/₄"

2¹/₂" 1¹/₂"

9¹/₂ (10, 10¹/₂, 11)"

Front and Back

23 (24, 24¹/₂, 25¹/₂)"

14 (14¹/₂, 14¹/₂, 15)"

2¹/₂"

21 (23³/₄, 26¹/₂, 29¹/₂)"

19 (20, 21, 22)"

Sleeve

17¹/₂ (17, 16¹/₄, 15³/₄)"

2¹/₂"

12¹/₄"

Woman's Tunic

INTERMEDIATE SKILL LEVEL

SIZES

Woman's Small (Medium, Large, Extra-Large). Instructions are for smallest size, with changes for other sizes noted in parentheses as necessary.

FINISHED MEASUREMENTS

Bust: 40 (45, 49, 54)"
Length: 26 (27, 27, 28)"
Sleeve width at underarm: 18 (19, 19, 20)"

MATERIALS

Lion Brand's *Wool-Ease* (worsted weight; 80% acrylic/20% wool; 3 oz; approx 197 yds), 9 (10, 11, 11) skeins Fisherman #099
Crochet hooks, sizes G/6 and H/8 or size needed to obtain gauge

GAUGE

With larger hook, 14 hdc and 11 rows = 4".
To measure your gauge, make a test swatch as follows: With larger hook, ch 15.
Foundation Row: Hdc into third ch from hook and into each ch across—14 hdc. Ch 2, turn.
Next Row: Skip first hdc, hdc into each hdc across, ending row with hdc into top of turning-ch-2. Ch 2, turn.
Repeat last row nine *more* times.
Fasten off.
Piece should measure 4" square. **To save time, take time to check gauge.**

NOTES

To decrease, work a dec hdc to combine the first 2 sts and/or the last 2 sts of the row.
Dec hdc = (Yarn over, insert hook into next st and pull up a loop) twice, yarn over and draw it through all five loops on hook.
To increase, work 2 sts into one st.
Each hdc, FPTR, FPDTR, and turning-ch-2 counts as one st.
FPTR and FPDTR are referred to as FPSTS.

CENTER PANEL

(Over middle 22 sts)
Foundation Row 1 (RS): FPTR into next 2 sts two rows below, skip the 2 hdc behind the 2 FPSTS just made, hdc into next 7 hdc, FPTR into next 4 sts two rows below, skip the 4 hdc behind the 4 FPSTS just made, hdc into next 7 hdc, FPTR into next 2 sts two rows below, skip the 2 hdc behind the 2 FPSTS just made.
Foundation Row 2: Hdc into each st across.
Row 1 (RS): FPTR into 2 FPSTS two rows below, skip the 2 hdc behind the 2 FPSTS just made, hdc into next 5 hdc, FPDTR into next 2 FPSTS two rows below, skip the 2 hdc behind the 2 FPSTS just made, hdc into next 4 hdc, FPDTR into next 2 FPSTS two rows below, skip the 2 hdc behind the 2 FPSTS just made, hdc into next 5 hdc, FPTR into next 2 FPSTS two rows below, skip the 2 hdc behind the 2 FPSTS just made.
Row 2 and all WS rows: Hdc into each st across.

Row 3: FPTR into next 2 FPSTS two rows below, skip the 2 hdc behind the 2 FPSTS just made, hdc into next 3 hdc, FPDTR into next 2 FPSTS two rows below, skip the 2 hdc behind the 2 FPSTS just made, hdc into next 8 hdc, FPDTR into next 2 FPSTS two rows below, skip the 2 hdc behind the 2 FPSTS just made, hdc into next 3 hdc, FPTR into the next 2 FPSTS two rows below, skip the 2 hdc behind the 2 FPSTS just made.
Row 5: FPTR into next 2 FPSTS two rows below, skip the 2 hdc behind the 2 FPSTS just made, hdc into next hdc, FPDTR into next 2 FPSTS two rows below, skip the 2 hdc behind the 2 FPSTS just made, hdc into next 4 hdc, FPTR into next 4 hdc two rows below, skip the 4 hdc behind the 4 FPSTS just made, hdc into next 4 hdc, FPDTR into the next 2 FPSTS two rows below, skip the 2 hdc behind the 2 FPSTS just made, hdc into next hdc, FPTR into next 2 FPSTS two rows below, skip the 2 hdc behind the 2 FPSTS just made.
Row 6: As Row 2.
Repeat Rows 1-6 for patt.

SIDEWAYS RIB PATT

(Over any number of ch)
Foundation Row: Sc into second ch from hook and into each ch across. Ch 1, turn.
Patt Row: Sc into the back loop of each sc across. Ch 1, turn.
Repeat Patt Row.

BACK

With larger hook, ch 73 (81, 89, 97).

Foundation Row 1 (RS): Hdc into third ch from hook and into each ch across—72 (80, 88, 96) sts. Ch 2, turn.

Foundation Row 2: Skip first hdc, hdc into each st across, ending row with hdc into top of turning-ch-2. Ch 2, turn.

Next Row (RS): Skip first hdc, hdc into next 24 (28, 32, 36) hdc, work Foundation Row 1 of Center Panel over middle 22 sts, work hdc into next 24 (28, 32, 36) hdc, ending row with hdc into top of turning-ch-2. Ch 2, turn.

Cont even as established, working middle 22 sts in Cable Panel with solid hdc on each side, until piece measures approx 17 (17$\frac{1}{2}$, 17$\frac{1}{2}$, 18)" from beg, ending after WS row. *Do not ch 2 to turn.*

Shape Armholes: Next Row (RS): Slip st into first 6 sts, ch 2, cont in patt as established across next 61 (69, 77, 85) sts. Ch 2, turn, leaving rest of row unworked.

Cont even until piece measures approx 25$\frac{1}{2}$ (26$\frac{1}{2}$, 26$\frac{1}{2}$, 27$\frac{1}{2}$)" from beg, ending after WS row. Ch 2, turn.

Shape Neck: Next Row (RS): Work across first 19 (23, 27, 31) sts, ch 2, turn, leaving rest of row unworked.

Next Row: Dec 1 st at neck edge, and work in patt to end row. Ch 2, turn.

Cont even if necessary until this side measures approx 26 (27, 27, 28)" from beg. Fasten off.

For second side of neck, with RS facing, skip the middle 24 sts and attach yarn with a slip st to next st and ch 2. Complete as for first side.

POCKET LININGS
(Make Two)
With larger hook, ch 18.

Foundation Row (RS): Hdc into third ch from hook and into each ch across—17 sts. Ch 2, turn.

Next Row: Skip first hdc, hdc into each st across, ending row with hdc into top of turning-ch-2. Ch 2, turn.

Repeat last row until piece measures approx 5" from beg, ending after WS row. Fasten off.

FRONT

Work as for back until piece measures approx 6" from beg, ending after WS row.

Place Pocket Linings: Next Row (RS): Work across first 4 (6, 8, 10) sts, work hdc into 17 hdc of one pocket lining, skip next 17 sts on front, cont in patt across next 30 (34, 38, 42) sts, work hdc into 17 hdc of second pocket lining, skip next 17 sts on front, work to end row.

Cont even until piece measures approx 23$\frac{1}{2}$ (24$\frac{1}{2}$, 24$\frac{1}{2}$, 25$\frac{1}{2}$)" from beg, ending after WS row. Ch 2, turn.

Shape Neck: Next Row (RS): Cont in patt as established, and work across first 22 (26, 30, 34) sts, ch 2, turn, leaving rest of row unworked. Dec 1 st at neck edge every row four times—18 (22, 26, 30) sts rem. Cont even on this side until it measures same as back to shoulders. Fasten off.

For second side of neck, with RS facing, skip the middle 18 sts, attach yarn with a slip st to next st and ch 2. Complete as for first side.

SLEEVES

With larger hook, ch 35.

Foundation Row 1 (RS): Hdc into third ch from hook and into each ch across—34 sts. Ch 2, turn.

Foundation Row 2: Skip first hdc, hdc into each st across, ending row with hdc into top of turning-ch-2. Ch 2, turn.

Next Row (RS): Skip first hdc, hdc into next 5 hdc, work Foundation Row 1 of Center Panel over middle 22 sts, work hdc into next 5 hdc, ending row with hdc into top of turning-ch-2. Ch 2, turn.

Cont as established, working middle 22 sts in Cable Panel with solid hdc on each side, and inc 1 st each side every other row 8 (13, 14, 19) times, then every fourth row 7 (4, 3, 0) times—64 (68, 68, 72) sts. Cont even until sleeve measures approx 19$\frac{1}{2}$ (19, 18$\frac{1}{4}$, 17$\frac{1}{2}$)" from beg. Fasten off.

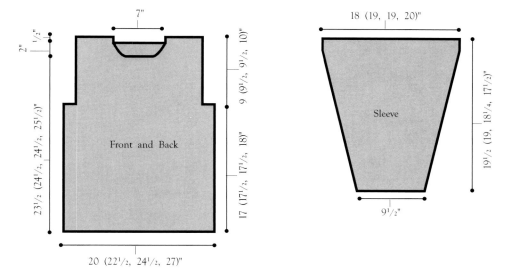

FINISHING

Sew shoulder seams.

Neckband: With RS facing and smaller hook, attach yarn with a slip st to neck edge of right shoulder seam and ch 1. Work 68 sc around neckline. Join with a slip st to first sc. Fasten off.

With smaller hook, ch 17. Work Sideways Rib Patt until piece, when slightly stretched, fits around neckline—16 sc each row. Fasten off. Sew foundation row of neckband to the last row of the neckband. Sewing through back loops of each sc, sew neck ribbing into place in neckline, placing seam at center of back neck.

Pocket Bands: With RS facing and smaller hook, attach yarn with a slip st to top of pocket edge and ch 1. Work 17 sc along top of pocket. Ch 1, turn.

Next Row: Sc into each sc. Fasten off.

Sew sides of pocket band to front. Sew pocket linings to WS of front.

Set in sleeves. Sew sleeve and side seams.

Girl's Poncho

INTERMEDIATE SKILL LEVEL

SIZES
Child's size 4-8 (10-14). Instructions are for smaller size, with changes for larger size noted in parentheses as necessary.

MATERIALS
Lion Brand's *Wool-Ease* (worsted weight, 80% acrylic/20% wool; 3 oz; approx 197 yds), 5 (6) skeins Fisherman #099
Crochet hooks, sizes G/6 and H/8 or size needed to obtain gauge

GAUGE
With larger hook, 16 hdc and 12 rows = 4".
To measure your gauge, make a test swatch as follows: With larger hook, ch 17.
Foundation Row: Hdc into third ch from hook and into each ch across—15 hdc plus turning-ch-2. Ch 2, turn.
Next Row: Skip first hdc, hdc into each hdc across, ending row with hdc into top of turning-ch-2. Ch 2, turn.
Repeat last row ten *more* times. Fasten off.
Piece should measure 4" square. **To save time, take time to check gauge.**

NOTES
Each turning-ch-2 counts as one hdc.
Tall Rope St = Yarn over hook, insert hook from front to back to front around the post of next st two rows below and pull up a loop, yarn over and draw it through 2 loops on hook; yarn over, insert hook from front to back to front of same st and pull up a loop, (yarn over and draw it through 2 loops on hook) three times. Always skip the hdc behind every tall rope st.

Popcorn = 5 dc into next st; remove loop from hook; insert hook from back to front in the first dc of the 5-dc group, replace loop onto hook and draw loop through the first dc.

STRIP
(Make Two)
With larger hook, ch 44 (56).

Foundation Row 1 (RS): Hdc into third ch from hook and into each ch across—43 (55) sts. Ch 2, turn.

Foundation Row 2: Skip first hdc, hdc into each hdc across, ending row with hdc into top of turning-ch-2—42 (54) hdc plus turning-ch-2. Ch 2, turn.

Row 1 (RS): Skip first hdc, hdc into next hdc, tall rope st, hdc into next hdc, tall rope st, *hdc into next 9 (13) sts, tall rope st, hdc into next hdc, tall rope st. Repeat from * across, ending row with hdc into next hdc, hdc into top of turning-ch-2. Ch 2, turn.

Row 2: Skip first hdc, hdc into next 6 sts, *(popcorn into next hdc, hdc into next 3 hdc) once (twice), popcorn into next hdc, hdc into next 7 sts. Repeat from * across, ending row with (popcorn into next hdc, hdc into next 3 hdc) once (twice), popcorn into next hdc, hdc into next 6 sts, hdc into top of turning-ch-2. Ch 2, turn.

Row 3: Same as Row 1. Ch 2, turn.

Row 4: Skip first hdc, *hdc into next 8 sts, (popcorn into next hdc, hdc into next 3 hdc) once (twice). Repeat from * across, ending row with hdc into next 5 sts, hdc into top of turning-ch-2. Ch 2, turn.

Repeat Rows 1-4 for patt until strip measures approx 24 (25)" from beg, ending after RS row. Fasten off.

FINISHING
Sew strips tog following illustration. On neck opening, mark both seams.

Neck Edging: With RS facing and smaller hook, attach yarn with a slip st to one seam and ch 1.

Rnd 1: Work one rnd of sc around neckline, working a dec sc where marked. Join with a slip st to first sc. Ch 1, do not turn.

Rnd 2: As Rnd 1. Join with a slip st to first sc. Fasten off.

With RS facing, attach fringe evenly along lower edges of poncho. Trim fringe evenly.

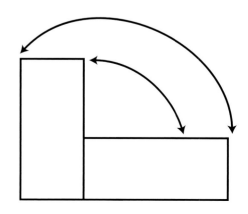

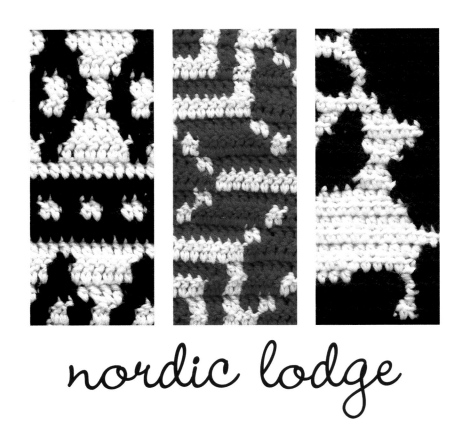

nordic lodge

Here's a collection of sweaters with something special for everyone in your family. You'll have fun watching the Nordic-inspired patterns emerge with each additional row.

Man's Reindeer Pullover

INTERMEDIATE SKILL LEVEL

SIZES
Man's Small (Medium, Large, Extra-Large). Instructions are for smallest size, with changes for other sizes noted in parentheses as necessary.

FINISHED MEASUREMENTS
Chest: 42$\frac{1}{2}$ (45$\frac{1}{2}$, 48$\frac{1}{2}$, 51$\frac{1}{2}$)"
Length: 27 (28, 28$\frac{1}{2}$, 29)"
Sleeve width at underarm: 19$\frac{1}{4}$ (20$\frac{1}{4}$, 21$\frac{1}{4}$, 22$\frac{1}{4}$)"

MATERIALS
Lion Brand's *Wool-Ease* (worsted weight, 80% acrylic/20% wool; 3 oz; approx 197 yds), 2 (2, 3, 4) skeins Fisherman #99 (A) and 8 (9, 9, 10) skeins Navy #111 (B)
Crochet hooks, sizes G/6 and H/8 or size needed to obtain gauge

GAUGE
With larger hook, in solid hdc, 16 hdc and 11 rows = 4".
To measure your gauge, make a test swatch as follows: With larger hook, ch 17.
Foundation Row: Hdc into third ch from hook and into each ch across—16 hdc total. Ch 2, turn.
Row 1: Skip first hdc, hdc into each st across, ending row with hdc into top of turning-ch-2. Ch 2, turn.
Repeat last row nine *more* times. Fasten off.
Piece should measure 4" square. **To save time, take time to check gauge.**

NOTES
To decrease, work a dec hdc to combine the first 2 sts and/or the last 2 sts of the row.
Dec hdc = (Yarn over, insert hook into next st and pull up a loop) twice, yarn over and draw it through all five loops on hook.
To increase, work 2 sts into one st.
To change color, work until 3 loops rem on hook; with the new color, complete the st; fasten off the old color. Each dc, FPDC, BPDC, hdc and turning-ch-2 counts as one st.

RIB PATT
(Over an odd number of ch)
Foundation Row (RS): Dc into fourth ch from hook and into each ch across. Ch 2, turn.
Row 1 (WS): Skip first st, *FPDC into next st, BPDC into next st. Repeat from * across, ending row with FPDC into next st, hdc into top of turning-ch. Ch 2, turn.
Row 2: Skip first st, *BPDC into next st, FPDC into next st. Repeat from *across, ending row with BPDC into next st, hdc into top of turning-ch-2. Ch 2, turn.
Repeat Rows 1 and 2 for patt.

REINDEER PATT
(Over 47 sts)
See chart, page 20.

BACK
With larger hook and A, ch 87 (93, 99, 105). Work Rib Patt until piece measures approx 2$\frac{1}{2}$" from beg, ending after WS row—85 (91, 97, 103) sts each row. Ch 2, turn.

Next Row (RS): Skip first st, hdc into each st across, ending row with hdc into top of turning-ch-2. Ch 2, turn.

Next Row (WS): Same as last row. Ch 2, turn.

Next Row (RS): Beg Border Chart, page 20. Ch 2, turn.

When Row 4 of Border Chart is completed, cont even with B until piece measures approx 17$\frac{1}{2}$ (18, 18, 18)" from beg, ending after WS row. Ch 2, turn.

Shape Armholes: Dec 1 st each side every row six times—73 (79, 85, 91) sts rem.

Work even until piece measures approx 26 (27, 27$\frac{1}{2}$, 28)" from beg, ending after WS row. Ch 2, turn.

Shape Neck: Next Row (RS): Skip first hdc, hdc into next 22 (25, 28, 31) sts, ch 2, turn, leaving rest of row unworked. Dec 1 st at neck edge every row twice—21 (24, 27, 30) sts rem. Cont even on this side until piece measures 27 (28, 28$\frac{1}{2}$, 29)" from beg. Fasten off.

For second side of neck, with RS facing, skip the middle 27 hdc, attach yarn with a slip st to next st and ch 2. Complete as for first side.

FRONT

Work as for back until piece measures approx 13 (13½, 14, 14½)" from beg, ending after WS row. Ch 2, turn.

Next Row (RS): Work across first 19 (22, 25, 28) hdc with B, work Row 1 of Reindeer Chart over middle 47 hdc, work hdc with B to end row. Ch 2, turn.

When piece measures same as back to armholes, **Shape Armholes** same as for back; when Row 26 of Reindeer Chart is completed, cont even with B until piece measures approx 24 (25, 25½, 26)" from beg, ending after WS row. Ch 2, turn.

Shape Neck: Next Row (RS): Skip first hdc, hdc into next 25 (28, 31, 34) sts, ch 2, turn, leaving rest of row unworked. Dec 1 st at neck edge every row five times—21 (24, 27, 30) sts rem. Cont even on this side until piece measures 27 (28, 28½, 29)" from beg. Fasten off.

For second side of neck, with RS facing, skip the middle 21 hdc and attach yarn with a slip st to next st and ch 2. Complete as for first side.

SLEEVES

With larger hook and A, ch 39 (41, 41, 43). Work Rib Patt until piece measures approx 2¹/₂" from beg, ending after WS row—37 (39, 39, 41) sts each row. Ch 2, turn.

Next Row (RS): Skip first st, hdc into each st across, inc 0 (4, 4, 2) sts evenly across, ending row with hdc into top of turning-ch-2—37 (43, 43, 43) hdc. Ch 2, turn.

Next Row: Skip first hdc, hdc into each hdc across, ending row with hdc into top of turning-ch-2. Ch 2, turn.

Next Row: Beg Border Chart, and inc 1 st each side every other row 18 (16, 19, 22) times, then inc 1 st each side every fourth row 2 (3, 2, 1) times—77 (81, 85, 89) sts. Cont even until sleeve measures approx 19³/₄ (19³/₄, 20, 20³/₄)" from beg, ending after WS row. Ch 2, turn.

Shape Cap: Dec 1 st each side every row six times—65 (69, 73, 77) sts rem. Fasten off.

FINISHING

Sew shoulder seams.

Neckband: With RS facing and smaller hook, attach B with a slip st to neck edge of right shoulder seam and ch 3.

Rnd 1: Work 85 dc evenly around neckline. Join with a slip st to top of ch-3—86 sts. Ch 2, do not turn.

Rnd 2: Skip first st, *FPDC into next st, BPDC into next st. Repeat from * around, ending rnd with FPDC, slip st to top of ch-2. Ch 2.

Repeat Rnd 2 until band measures approx 1" from beg. Fasten off.

Set in sleeves. Sew sleeve and side seams.

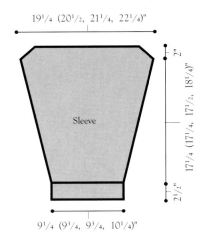

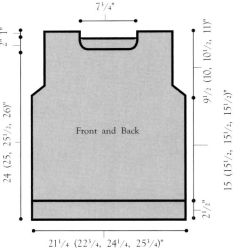

Reindeer Chart

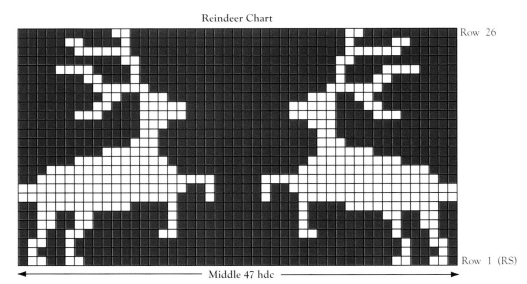

Row 26

Row 1 (RS)

◄———— Middle 47 hdc ————►

Border Chart

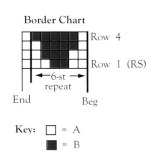

Row 4

Row 1 (RS)

◄—6-st repeat—►

End   Beg

Key: ☐ = A
     ■ = B

Note: Each square on chart represents one hdc or turning-ch-2.

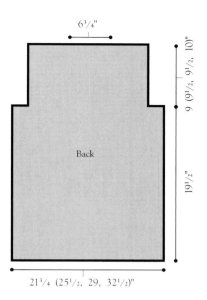

Woman's Fair Isle Jacket

ADVANCED SKILL LEVEL

SIZES

Woman's Small (Medium, Large, Extra-Large). Instructions are for smallest size, with changes for other sizes noted in parentheses as necessary.

FINISHED MEASUREMENTS

Bust (Buttoned): 45¼ (53, 59½, 67)"
Length: 28½ (29, 29, 29½)"
Sleeve width at underarm: 18 (19, 19, 20)"

MATERIALS

Lion Brand's *Wool-Ease* (worsted weight, 80% acrylic/20% wool; 3 oz; approx 197 yds), 6 (7, 8, 9) skeins Navy #111 (A) and 6 (7, 8, 8) skeins Fisherman #99 (B)
Crochet hook, size H/8 or size needed to obtain gauge
Six ¾" buttons (JHB International's *Oakwood Style #50952* was used on sample garment)

GAUGE

In Fair Isle Patt, 18 dc and 9 rows = 4".
To measure your gauge, make a test swatch as follows: With A, ch 20.
Foundation Row: Dc into fourth ch from hook and into each ch across—18 dc total. Ch 3, turn.
Next Row: Work Row 1 of Fair Isle Chart. Ch 3, turn.
Cont with chart through Row 8. Fasten off.
Piece should measure 4" square. **To save time, take time to check gauge.**

NOTES

To decrease, work a dec dc to combine the first 2 sts and/or the last 2 sts of the row.
To increase, work 2 sts into one st.
Dec dc = (Yarn over, insert hook into next st and pull up a loop, yarn over and draw it through two loops on hook) twice, yarn over and draw it through all three loops on hook.
Each dc and turning-ch-3 counts as one st.
To change color, work until 2 loops rem on hook; with the new color, complete the st; fasten off the old color.

FAIR ISLE PATT

See chart, page 22.

BACK

With A, ch 100 (116, 132, 148).

Foundation Row (RS): Dc into fourth ch from hook and into each ch across—98 (114, 130, 146) sts. Ch 3, turn. This completes Row 1 of Woman's Fair Isle Chart.

Cont Woman's Fair Isle Patt, and work even on 98 (114, 130, 146) sts until piece measures approx 19½" from beg, ending after Row 11 of chart. Fasten off B.

Shape Armholes: Next Row (RS): With RS facing, skip first 9 (9, 14, 14) sts, attach A with a slip st to next st and ch 3. Cont in patt as established across row, leaving last 9 (9, 14, 14) sts unworked—80 (96, 102, 118) sts.

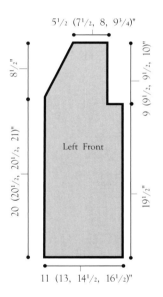

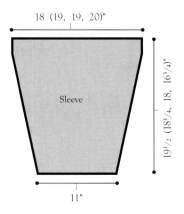

Work even until piece measures approx 28½ (29, 29, 29½)" from beg. Fasten off.

POCKET LININGS
(Make Two)
With B, ch 25.

Foundation Row: Sc into second ch from hook and into each ch across—24 sc. Ch 1, turn.

Next Row: Sc into each sc across. Ch 1, turn.

Repeat last row until piece measures approx 4½" from beg. Fasten off.

LEFT FRONT
With A, ch 52 (60, 68, 76).

Foundation Row (RS): Dc into fourth ch from hook and into each ch across—50 (58, 66, 74) sts. Ch 3, turn. This completes Row 1 of Woman's Fair Isle Chart.

Cont Woman's Fair Isle Patt, and work even on 50 (58, 66, 74) sts until piece measures approx 4¾" from beg, ending after Row 11 of patt.

Place Pocket Lining: Next Row (RS): Work patt across first 13 (17, 21, 25) sts, cont in Woman's Fair Isle Patt across 24 sts of one pocket lining, skip next 24 sts of left front, work to end row.

Cont even until piece measures same as back to armholes, ending after Row 11 of chart. Fasten off B.

Shape Armhole: Next Row (RS): With RS facing, skip first 9 (9, 14, 14) sts, attach A with a slip st to next st and ch 3. Cont in patt as established to end row— 41 (49, 52, 60) sts.

Cont even until piece measures 20 (20½, 20½, 21)" from beg, ending after RS row.

Shape Neck: Cont in patt and dec 1 st at neck edge every row sixteen times—25 (33, 36, 44) sts rem. Cont even until piece measures same as back. Fasten off.

RIGHT FRONT
Work same as left front, *except* reverse all shaping.

SLEEVES
With A, ch 52.

Foundation Row (RS): Dc into fourth ch from hook and into each ch across—50 sts. Ch 3, turn. This completes Row 1 of Woman's Fair Isle Chart.

Cont Woman's Fair Isle Patt, and inc 1 st each side every row 0 (4, 4, 10) times, then inc 1 st each side every other row 12 (14, 14, 10) times, then every fourth row 3 (0, 0, 0) times—80 (86, 86, 90) sts—working new sts into Fair Isle Patt. Cont even until piece measures approx 19½ (18¼, 18, 16¾)" from beg. Fasten off.

FINISHING
Sew shoulder seams.

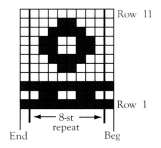

Row 11

Row 1

8-st repeat

End Beg

Key: ■ = A
□ = B

Note: Each square on chart represents one dc or turning-ch-3.

Base Row for Buttonhole Band: With RS facing, attach A with a slip st to lower right front edge and ch 1. Work 72 (74, 74, 76) sc along right front edge up to beg of front neck shaping, then work 42 sc along side of neckline to shoulder seam, working Navy sc in Navy areas and Fisherman sc in Fisherman areas— 114 (116, 116, 118) sc total. Fasten off.

Base Row for Buttonband: With RS facing, attach A with a slip st to left shoulder seam and ch 1. Work 42 sc along left front neck shaping, using corresponding section of right front for color reference, then work 72 (74, 74, 76) sc along left front edge down to lower edge, matching colors to sides of front—114 (116, 116, 118) sc total. Fasten off.

Collar: With RS facing, attach A with a slip st to neck edge of right shoulder seam and ch 1.

Row 1 (RS): Work 30 sc along back of neck; work sc into 3 sc of left front. Ch 1, turn.

Row 2: Sc into next 33 sc, sc into 3 sc of right front. Ch 1, turn.

Rows 3-28: Cont in sc, and work 3 additional sc on each sweater front each side every row—114 sc total. Fasten off.

Front Bands: With RS facing, attach A with a slip st to lower right front edge and ch 1. Work 72 (74, 74, 76) sc along right front edge, work 114 sc around collar, then work 72 (74, 74, 76) sc along left front edge—258 (262, 262, 266) sc total. Ch 1, turn.

Cont even until bands measures ³/₄" from beg. Place markers for six evenly-spaced buttonholes along right front edge, making the first and last ¹/₂" from beg of neck shaping and bottom edge.

Next Row: Cont in sc, and make six buttonholes where marked by working (ch 3, skip next 3 sc).

On next row, work 3 sc into each ch-3 sp of previous row.

Cont even until bands measure approx 1¹/₂" from beg. Fasten off.

Pocket Bands: With RS facing, attach A with a slip st to top of pocket edge and ch 1. Work 24 sc along top of pocket. Ch 1, turn.

Next Row: Sc into each sc. Fasten off.

Sew sides of pocket band to front. Sew pocket linings to WS of front.

Set in sleeves. Sew sleeve and side seams. Sew on buttons.

Child's Snowflake Pullover

INTERMEDIATE SKILL LEVEL

SIZES
Child's size 2 (4, 6, 8). Instructions are for smallest size, with changes for other sizes noted in parentheses as necessary.

FINISHED MEASUREMENTS
Chest: 27 (30, 32^1/$_2$, 35)"
Length: 15 (16, 17^1/$_2$, 19)"
Sleeve width at underarm: 13 (13^1/$_2$, 14^1/$_2$, 16)"

MATERIALS
Lion Brand's *Wool-Ease Sportweight* (sport weight, 80% acrylic/20% wool; 5 oz; approx 435 yds), 2 (2, 3, 3) skeins Ranch Red #102 (A) and 1 skein Fisherman #099 (B)
Crochet hooks, sizes E/4 and F/5 or size needed to obtain gauge

GAUGE
With larger hook, 20 dc and 11 rows = 4".
To measure your gauge, make a test swatch as follows: With larger hook, ch 22.
Foundation Row: Dc into fourth ch from hook and into each ch across—20 dc. Ch 3, turn.
Next Row: Skip first dc, dc into each dc across, ending row with dc into top of turning-ch-3. Ch 3, turn.
Repeat last row nine *more* times. Fasten off.
Piece should measure 4" square. **To save time, take time to check gauge.**

NOTES
Each turning-ch-2 counts as 1 hdc; each turning-ch-3 counts as 1 dc.
To decrease in dc, work until 2 sts rem in row, then work a dec dc to combine the last 2 sts in row. On the next row, work last st into the last dc, not into the top of the turning-ch-3.
Dec dc = (Yarn over, insert hook into next st and pull up a loop, yarn over and draw it through two loops on hook) twice, yarn over and draw it through all three loops on hook.
To increase, work 2 sts into one st.
To change color, work until 2 loops rem on hook; with the new color, complete the st; fasten off the old color.

RIB PATT
(Over an even number of ch)
Foundation Row (RS): Dc into fourth ch from hook and into each ch across. Ch 2, turn.
Row 1 (WS): Skip first st, *FPDC into next st, BPDC into next st. Repeat from * across, ending row with hdc into top of turning-ch. Ch 2, turn.
Row 2: Skip first st, *FPDC into next st, BPDC into next st. Repeat from * across, ending row with hdc into top of turning-ch-2. Ch 2, turn.
Repeat Rows 1 and 2 for patt.

SNOWFLAKE PATT
(Over 38 sts)
See chart, page 26.

BACK
With smaller hook and A, ch 70 (78, 84, 90). Work Rib Patt until piece measures approx 1^1/$_4$ (1^1/$_2$, 1^1/$_2$, 2)" from beg—68 (76, 82, 88) sts each row. Change to larger hook, ch 3, turn.

Next Row: Skip first st, dc into each st across, ending row with dc into top of turning-ch. Ch 3, turn.

Repeat last row until piece measures approx 8^1/$_2$ (9^1/$_4$, 10^1/$_4$, 11)" from beg. *Do not ch 3 to turn.*

Shape Armholes: Slip st into first 6 sts, ch 3, cont across until 5 sts rem in row. Ch 3, turn, leaving rest of row unworked—58 (66, 72, 78) dc.

Work even until piece measures approx 14^1/$_2$ (15^1/$_2$, 17, 18^1/$_2$)" from beg, ending after WS row. Ch 3, turn.

Shape Neck: Next Row (RS): Skip first dc, dc into next 14 (18, 20, 23) dc. Fasten off.

For second side of neck, with RS facing, skip the middle 28 (28, 30, 30) dc, attach yarn with a slip st to next dc and ch 3. Work dc into next 13 (17, 19, 22) dc, dc into top of turning-ch-3. Fasten off.

FRONT
Work as for back until piece measures approx 4^1/$_2$ (5^1/$_2$, 6^1/$_2$, 7^1/$_2$)" from beg. Ch 3, turn.

Next Row: Skip first dc, dc into next 14 (18, 21, 24) dc, work Row 1 of Snowflake Chart over middle 38 dc, work dc with A to end row.

Cont in dc, working Snowflake Chart over middle 38 dc until piece measures approx 8½ (9¼, 10¼, 11)" from beg. *Do not ch 3 to turn.*

Shape Armholes: Slip st into first 6 sts, ch 3, cont across until 5 sts rem in row. Ch 3, turn, leaving rest of row unworked—58 (66, 72, 78) dc.

Work even, using A after Row 19 of chart is completed, until piece measures approx 13 (14, 15½, 17)" from beg, ending after WS row. Ch 3, turn.

Shape Neck: Next Row (RS): Skip first dc, dc into next 17 (21, 23, 26) dc, ch 3, turn, leaving rest of row unworked. Dec 1 st at neck edge every row three times—15 (19, 21, 24) sts rem. Cont even until this side measures same as back to shoulders. Fasten off.

For second side of neck, with RS facing, skip the middle 22 (22, 24, 24) dc, attach yarn with a slip st to next dc and ch 3. Work dc into next 16 (20, 22, 25) dc, dc into top of turning-ch-3. Complete as for first side.

SLEEVES

With smaller hook and A, ch 36 (36, 38, 40). Work Rib Patt until piece measures approx 1¼ (1½, 1½, 2)" from beg—34 (34, 36, 38) sts each row. Change to larger hook, ch 3, turn.

Next Row: Skip first st, dc into each st across, ending row with 2 dc into top of turning-ch-3—35 (35, 37, 39) sts. Ch 3, turn.

Repeat last row, and inc 1 st each side every row 6 (6, 6, 12) times, then every other row 9 (10, 12, 9) times—65 (67, 73, 81) sts. Cont even until sleeve measures approx 11½ (13½, 14½, 14¾)" from beg. Fasten off.

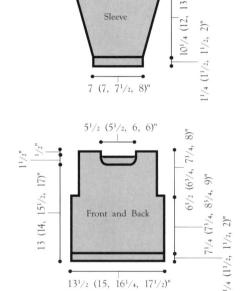

FINISHING

Sew shoulder seams.

Neckband: With RS facing and smaller hook, attach A with a slip st to neck edge of right shoulder seam and ch 3.

Rnd 1 (RS): Work 71 (71, 75, 75) dc evenly around neckline. Join with a slip st to top of ch-3—72 (72, 76, 76) sts. Ch 2, do not turn.

Rnd 2: Skip first st, *FPDC into next st, BPDC into next st. Repeat from * around, ending rnd with FPDC, slip st to top of ch-2. Ch 2.

Repeat last rnd once (once, twice, twice) *more*. Fasten off.

Set in sleeves. Sew sleeve and side seams.

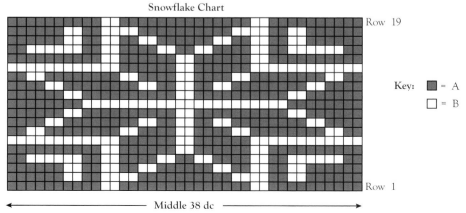

Snowflake Chart

Key: ■ = A
□ = B

Row 19

Row 1

◄—— Middle 38 dc ——►

Note: Each square on chart represent one dc.

Baby's Two-Piece Set

INTERMEDIATE SKILL LEVEL

SIZES

Infant's size 6 (12, 18) months. Instructions are for smallest size, with changes for other sizes noted in parentheses as necessary.

FINISHED MEASUREMENTS

Chest: 22 (24$\frac{1}{2}$, 27)"
Length: 11$\frac{1}{4}$ (12$\frac{1}{4}$, 13$\frac{1}{4}$)"
Sleeve width at underarm: 9 (10, 10$\frac{1}{2}$)"
Pants length: 16 (17, 18)"

MATERIALS

Lion Brand's *Jamie 3-Ply Baby* (sport weight, 100% Acrilan® acrylic; 1$\frac{3}{4}$ oz; approx 196 yds), 7 (7, 8) skeins Fisherman #299 (A) and
1 skein Scarlet #213 (B)
Crochet hooks, sizes D/3 and E/4 or size needed to obtain gauge
Four $\frac{1}{2}$" buttons (JHB International's *Classic Pearl Style #70165* was used on sample garment)
$\frac{3}{4}$" wide elastic measured to fit baby's waist

GAUGE

With larger hook, 24 hdc and 16 rows = 4".
To measure your gauge, make a test swatch as follows: With larger hook, ch 25.
Foundation Row: Hdc into third ch from hook and into each ch across—24 hdc. Ch 2, turn.

Next Row: Skip first hdc, hdc into each hdc across, ending row with hdc into top of turning-ch-2. Ch 2, turn.
Repeat last row fourteen *more* times.
Fasten off.
Piece should measure 4" square. **To save time, take time to check gauge.**

NOTES

Each turning-ch-3 counts as 1 dc; each turning-ch-2 counts as 1 hdc.
To decrease in hdc, work until 2 sts rem in row, then work a dec hdc to combine the last 2 sts in row. On the next row, work last st into the last hdc, not into the top of the turning-ch-2.
Dec hdc = (Yarn over, insert hook into next st and pull up a loop) twice, yarn over and draw it through all five loops on hook.
To increase, work 2 sts into one st.
To change color, work until 3 loops rem on hook; with the new color, complete the st; fasten off the old color.

RIB PATT

(Over an even number of ch)
Foundation Row (RS): Dc into fourth ch from hook and into each ch across. Ch 2, turn.
Patt Row: Skip first st, *FPDC into next st, BPDC into next st. Repeat from * across, ending row with hdc into top of turning-ch. Ch 2, turn.
Repeat Patt Row.

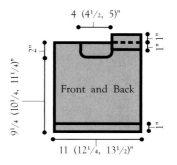

4 (4$\frac{1}{2}$, 5)"
2"
1" 1"
9$\frac{1}{4}$ (10$\frac{1}{4}$, 11$\frac{1}{4}$)"
Front and Back
1"
11 (12$\frac{1}{4}$, 13$\frac{1}{2}$)"

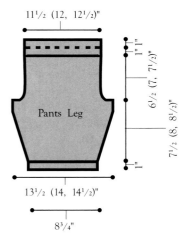

11$\frac{1}{2}$ (12, 12$\frac{1}{2}$)"
1" 1"
6$\frac{1}{2}$ (7, 7$\frac{1}{2}$)"
7$\frac{1}{2}$ (8, 8$\frac{1}{2}$)"
Pants Leg
1"
13$\frac{1}{2}$ (14, 14$\frac{1}{2}$)"
8$\frac{3}{4}$"

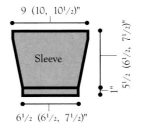

9 (10, 10$\frac{1}{2}$)"
5$\frac{1}{2}$ (6$\frac{1}{2}$, 7$\frac{1}{2}$)"
Sleeve
1"
6$\frac{1}{2}$ (6$\frac{1}{2}$, 7$\frac{1}{2}$)"

FAIR ISLE PATT
(Mult. 7 + 4 sts)
See chart.

PULLOVER BACK
With smaller hook and A, ch 68 (76, 82). Work Rib Patt for four rows total—66 (74, 80) sts each row. Change to larger hook, ch 2, turn.

Next Row (RS): Skip first st, hdc into each st across, ending row with 2 (1, 2) hdc into top of turning-ch-2—67 (74, 81) hdc. Ch 2, turn.

Next Row: Skip first st, hdc into each hdc across, ending row with hdc into top of turning-ch-2. Ch 2, turn.

Work Rows 1-8 of Baby's Fair Isle Chart. Cont even with A until piece measures approx 11¼ (12¼, 13¼)" from beg. Fasten off.

PULLOVER FRONT
Work as for back until piece measures approx 9¼ (10¼, 11¼)" from beg, ending after RS row. Ch 2, turn.

Shape Neck: Next Row (WS): Skip first hdc, hdc into next 23 (25, 27) hdc, ch 2, turn, leaving rest of row unworked. Dec 1 st at neck edge every row three times—21 (23, 25) sts rem. Cont even until this side measures same as back to shoulders. Fasten off.

For second side of neck, with WS facing, skip the middle 19 (22, 25) hdc, attach yarn with a slip st to next hdc and ch 2. Work hdc into next 22 (24, 26) hdc, hdc into top of turning-ch-2. Complete same as first side.

PULLOVER SLEEVES
With smaller hook and A, ch 40 (40, 48). Work Rib Patt for four rows total—38 (38, 46) sts each row. Change to larger hook, ch 2, turn.

Next Row (RS): Skip first st, hdc into each st across, ending row with 2 (2, 1) hdc into top of turning-ch-2—39 (39, 46) sts. Ch 2, turn.

Cont in hdc, and inc 1 st each side every other row 7 (11, 5) times, then every fourth row 1 (0, 4) times—55 (61, 64) sts. Cont even until sleeve measures approx 6½ (7½, 8½)" from beg. Fasten off.

PULLOVER FINISHING
Sew right shoulder seam.

Neckband: With RS facing and smaller hook, attach A with a slip st to left front neck edge and ch 3.

Row 1: Work 63 (67, 71) dc evenly around neckline, ending when 21 (23, 25) hdc rem unworked on back for left shoulder—64 (68, 72) sts including ch-3. Ch 2, turn.

Work three rows of Rib Patt. Fasten off.

Baby's Fair Isle Chart

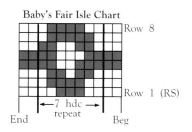

Row 8

Row 1 (RS)

←7 hdc→
repeat

End   Beg

Key: ☐ = A
▨ = B

Note: Each square on chart represents one hdc or turning-ch-2.

Button Band: With RS facing and smaller hook, attach A with a slip st to side of back left neckband and ch 3.

Row 1: Work 4 dc along side of neckband, then work 21 (23, 25) dc along left back shoulder—26 (28, 30) sts, including ch-3. Ch 2, turn.

Work three rows of Rib Patt. Fasten off. Place markers for four evenly-spaced buttons along button band.

Buttonhole Band: With RS facing and smaller hook, attach A with a slip st to shoulder edge of front and ch 3.

Row 1: Skip first st, work 20 (22, 24) dc along right front shoulder, then work 5 dc along side of neckband—26 (28, 30) sts, including ch-3. Ch 2, turn.

Work one row of Rib Patt. Ch 2, turn.

Next Row: Cont in rib as established, and work buttonholes opposite markers by working (ch 1, skip next st). Complete same as button band.

Overlap buttonhole band over button band and sew armhole edge of bands tog. Place markers 4¹/₂ (5, 5¹/₄)" down from shoulders. Set in sleeves between markers. Sew sleeve and side seams. Sew on buttons.

PANTS LEGS
(Make Two)
With smaller hook and A, ch 54. Work Rib Patt for four rows total—52 sts each row. Change to larger hook, ch 2, turn.

Next Row (RS): Skip first st, hdc into each st across, ending row with 2 hdc into top of turning-ch-2—53 sts. Ch 2, turn.

Next Row: Skip first st, hdc into each hdc across, ending row with hdc into top of turning-ch-2. Ch 2, turn.

Cont in hdc, and inc 1 st each side every row 2 (4, 4) times, then every other row 12 (12, 13) times—81 (85, 87) sts.

Work even until piece measures approx 8¹/₂ (9, 9¹/₂)" from beg, ending after WS row. *Do not ch 2 to turn.*

Shape Crotch: **Next Row (RS):** Slip st into first 3 sts, ch 2, hdc into next 76 (80, 82) sts. Ch 2, turn, leaving rest of row unworked—77 (81, 83) sts.

Dec 1 st each side every row four times—69 (73, 75) sts.

Cont even until piece measures 14³/₄ (15³/₄, 16³/₄)" from beg, ending after RS row.

Next Row (WS): Dec 1 st, hdc across—68 (72, 74) sts. Fasten off.

PANTS FINISHING
Sew inside leg seams. Sew center front and back seams.

Waistband: With RS facing and smaller hook, attach A with a slip st to back seam and ch 3.

Rnd 1: Work 135 (143, 149) dc evenly around waistline—136 (144, 150) sts total, including ch-3. Slip st to top of ch-3. Ch 2, do not turn.

Rnd 2: Skip first st, *FPDC into next st, BPDC into next st. Repeat from * around, ending rnd with FPDC into next st, slip st to top of ch-2. Ch 2.

Repeat last rnd until waistband measures approx 2" from beg. Fasten off.

Fold waistband in half to WS and sew into place to form a casing, leaving an opening for elastic. Cut elastic to fit baby's waist with ¹/₂" overlap. Slip elastic through casing, and sew ends tog securely. Sew casing closed.

casual and carefree

Refresh your family's summer wardrobe with these softly-colored designs.

Man's Textured Crewneck Pullover

INTERMEDIATE SKILL LEVEL

SIZES

Man's Small (Medium, Large, Extra-Large). Instructions are for smallest size, with changes for other sizes noted in parentheses as necessary.

FINISHED MEASUREMENTS

Chest: 43 (46½, 49½, 53)"
Length: 26 (27, 27½, 28)"
Sleeve width at underarm: 19 (20, 21, 22)"

MATERIALS

Coats and Clark's *Red Heart Soft* (heavy worsted weight, 100% acrylic with Bounce-Back® fibers; 5 oz; approx 328 yds), 7 (8, 8, 9) skeins Medium Blue #7821
Crochet hooks, sizes G/6 and H/8 or size needed to obtain gauge

GAUGE

With larger hook, in Textured Patt, 20 sts and 12 rows = 4".
To measure your gauge, make a test swatch as follows: With larger hook, ch 21.
Work even in Textured Patt for twelve rows total. Fasten off.
Piece should measure 4" square. **To save time, take time to check gauge.**

NOTES

To decrease, work a dec hdc to combine the first 2 sts and/or the last 2 sts of the row.
Dec hdc = (Yarn over, insert hook into next st and pull up a loop) twice, yarn over and draw it through all five loops on hook.
To increase, work 2 sts into one st.
Each hdc and turning-ch-2 counts as one st.

RIB PATT

(Over an even number of ch)
Foundation Row (RS): Dc into fourth ch from hook and into each ch across. Ch 2, turn.
Row 1 (WS): Skip first st, *FPDC into next st, BPDC into next st. Repeat from * across, ending row with hdc into top of turning-ch. Ch 2, turn.
Row 2: Skip first st, *FPDC into next st, BPDC into next st. Repeat from * across, ending row with hdc into top of turning-ch-2. Ch 2, turn.
Repeat Rows 1 and 2 for patt.

TEXTURED PATT

(Over an even number of sts)
Foundation Row (RS): Hdc into third ch from hook and into each ch across—20 sts total. Ch 2, turn.
Patt Row: Skip first hdc, *hdc *into back loop only* of next st, hdc *into front loop only* of next st. Repeat from * across, ending row with hdc into top of turning-ch-2. Ch 2, turn.
Repeat Patt Row.

BACK

With smaller hook, ch 110 (118, 126, 134). Work Rib Patt until piece measures approx 3" from beg, ending after WS row—108 (116, 124, 132) sts each row. Ch 2, turn.

Change to larger hook, beg Textured Patt and work even until piece measures approx 16½ (17, 17, 17)" from beg, ending after WS row. *Do not ch 2 to turn.*

Shape Armholes: Slip st into first 9 (9, 11, 11) sts, ch 2, cont in Textured Patt across next 91 (99, 103, 111) sts as established. Ch 2, turn, leaving rest of row unworked—92 (100, 104, 112) sts rem.

Work even until piece measures approx 26 (27, 27½, 28)" from beg. Fasten off.

FRONT

Work as for back until piece measures approx 23 (24, 24½, 25)" from beg, ending after WS row. Ch 2, turn.

Shape Neck: Next Row (RS): Work in patt as established across first 33 (37, 39, 43) sts. Ch 2, turn, leaving rest of row unworked.

Dec 1 st at neck edge every row seven times—26 (30, 32, 36) sts rem.

Cont even until this side measures same as back to shoulders. Fasten off.

For second side of neck, with RS facing, skip the middle 26 sts and attach yarn with a slip st to next st and ch 2. Complete as for first side.

SLEEVES

With smaller hook, ch 50 (50, 52, 52). Work Rib Patt until piece measures approx 3" from beg, ending after WS row—48 (48, 50, 50) sts each row. Ch 2, turn.

Change to larger hook, beg Textured Patt, and inc 1 st each side every row 2 (6, 12, 14) times, then every other row 21 (20, 15, 16) times, working new sts into patt as established—94 (100, 104, 110) sts.

Cont even until piece measures approx $21\frac{1}{4}$ ($21\frac{1}{2}$, $21\frac{1}{2}$, $21\frac{3}{4}$)" from beg. Fasten off.

FINISHING

Sew shoulder seams.

Neckband: With RS facing and smaller hook, attach yarn with a slip st to neck edge of right shoulder seam and ch 3.

Rnd 1: Work 107 dc evenly around neckline. Join with a slip st to top of ch-3. Ch 2, do not turn.

Rnd 2: Skip first st, *FPDC into next st, BPDC into next st. Repeat from * around, ending rnd with FPDC, slip st to top of ch-2. Ch 2.

Repeat Rnd 2 until band measures approx 1" from beg. Fasten off.

Set in sleeves. Sew sleeve and side seams.

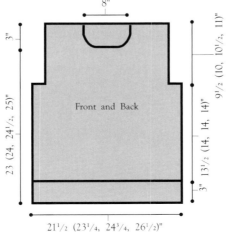

8"

3"

$9\frac{1}{2}$ (10, $10\frac{1}{2}$, 11)"

23 (24, $24\frac{1}{2}$, 25)"

Front and Back

$13\frac{1}{2}$ (14, 14, 14)"

3"

$21\frac{1}{2}$ ($23\frac{1}{4}$, $24\frac{3}{4}$, $26\frac{1}{2}$)"

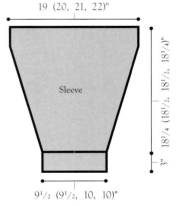

19 (20, 21, 22)"

Sleeve

$18\frac{1}{4}$ ($18\frac{1}{2}$, $18\frac{1}{2}$, $18\frac{3}{4}$)"

3"

$9\frac{1}{2}$ ($9\frac{1}{2}$, 10, 10)"

Woman's Rose Vest

INTERMEDIATE SKILL LEVEL

SIZES
Woman's Small (Medium, Large, Extra-Large). Instructions are for smallest size, with changes for other sizes noted in parentheses as necessary.

FINISHED MEASUREMENTS
Bust (Buttoned): 37 (42, 47, 52)"
Length (Excluding Edging): 21½ (22, 22, 22½)"

MATERIALS
Coats and Clark's *Lustersheen* (fingering weight, 100% acrylic; 1⅘ oz; approx 150 yds), 8 (8, 9, 10) balls Crystal Pink #206
Crochet hook, sizes D/3 and E/4 or size needed to obtain gauge
Six ¾" buttons (JHB International's *Anaheim Style #44868* was used on sample garment)

GAUGE
With larger hook, in Striped Lace Patt, 26 sts and 13 rows = 4".
To measure your gauge, make a test swatch as follows: With larger hook, ch 31.
Foundation Row (RS): Dc into fourth ch from hook and into each ch across—29 sts. Ch 4, turn.
Next Row (WS): Skip first 2 dc, *dc into next dc, ch 1, skip next dc. Repeat from * across, ending row with dc into top of turning-ch-3. Ch 3, turn.

Next Row: Skip first dc, *dc into next ch-1 sp, dc into next dc. Repeat from * across, ending row with dc under turning-ch-4, dc into third ch of turning-ch-4. Ch 4, turn.
Repeat last two rows five *more* times. Fasten off.
Piece should measure 4½" wide and 4" long. **To save time, take time to check gauge.**

NOTES
In Striped Lace Patt, each dc and turning-ch-3 counts as one st; each turning-ch-4 counts as two sts.
To make a dec dc into turning-ch at the end of RS rows in Striped Lace Patt: yarn over, insert hook under turning-ch and pull up a loop, yarn over and draw it through two loops on hook; yarn over, insert hook into third ch of turning-ch and pull up a loop, yarn over and draw it through two loops on hook; yarn over and draw through all three loops on hook.
Dec sc = (Insert hook into next st and pull up a loop) twice, yarn over and draw it through all three loops on hook.

LACY SQUARES PATT
(Ch mult. 8 + 1)
Foundation Row (RS): Sc into thirteenth ch from hook, *ch 3, turn; 5 dc into ch-sp just made, ch 3, turn; skip first dc, dc into next 4 dc, dc into top of turning-ch-3, skip next 3 ch of foundation ch, dc into next ch, ch 5, skip next 3 ch of foundation ch, sc into next ch. Repeat from * across, ending row with ch 3, turn; 5 dc into ch-sp just made, ch 3, turn; skip first dc, dc into next 4 dc, dc into top of turning-ch-3, skip next 3 ch of foundation ch, dc into next ch. Ch 7, turn.

Row 1 (WS): Skip first 6 dc, *sc into top of next ch-3, ch 4, dc into next dc, ch 4, skip next 5 dc. Repeat from * across, ending row with sc into top of next ch-3, ch 4, dc under turning-ch. Ch 7, turn.
Row 2: *Sc into next sc, ch 4, dc into next dc, ch 4. Repeat from * across, ending row with sc into next sc, ch 4, dc into third ch of turning-ch. Ch 7, turn.
Row 3: As Row 2. Ch 8, turn.
Row 4: *Sc into next sc, ch 3, turn; 5 dc into ch-sp just made, ch 3, turn; skip first dc, dc into next 4 dc, dc into top of turning-ch-3, dc into next dc of previous row, ch 5. Repeat from * across, ending row with sc into next sc, ch 3, turn; 5 dc into ch-sp just made, ch 3, turn; skip first dc, dc into next 4 dc, dc into top of turning-ch-3, dc into third ch of turning-ch. Ch 7, turn.
Repeat Rows 1-4 for patt.

STRIPED LACE PATT
(Over an odd number of sts)
Row 1 (RS): Skip first dc, *dc into next ch-1 sp, dc into next dc. Repeat from * across, ending row with dc under turning-ch-4, dc into third ch of turning-ch. Ch 4, turn.
Row 2 (WS): Skip first 2 dc, *dc into next dc, ch 1, skip next dc. Repeat from * across, ending row with dc into top of turning-ch-3. Ch 3, turn.
Repeat Rows 1 and 2 for patt.

BACK
With larger hook, ch 129 (145, 161, 177). Beg Lacy Squares Patt, and work even until piece measures approx 11½" from beg, ending after Row 2 of patt. Ch 4, turn.

Next Row (WS): Skip first dc, *dc into next ch-4 sp, ch 1, dc into next st, ch 1. Repeat from * across, ending row with dc under turning-ch-7, ch 1, dc into third ch of turning-ch-7—121 (137, 153, 169) sts. Ch 3, turn.

Next Row: Work as for Row 1 of Striped Lace Patt. *Do not ch 4 to turn.*

Shape Armholes: Next Row (WS): Slip st into first 23 (27, 31, 37) sts, ch 4, *skip next dc, dc into next dc, ch 1. Repeat from * across until 22 (26, 30, 36) sts rem. Ch 3, turn, leaving rest of row unworked—77 (85, 93, 97) sts.

Cont even in Striped Lace Patt until piece measures approx 20 (20½, 20½, 21)" from beg, ending after Row 1 of Striped Lace Patt.

Shape Neck: Next Row (WS): Work patt as established across first 15 (19, 23, 25) sts, ch 3, turn, leaving rest of row unworked.

Cont even in patt as established on these 15 (19, 23, 25) sts until this side measures approx 21½ (22, 22, 22½)" from beg. Fasten off.

For second side of neck, with WS facing, skip the middle 47 sts, attach yarn with a slip st to next st and ch 4. Skip next dc, *dc into next dc, ch 1, skip next dc. Repeat from * across, ending row with dc into top of turning-ch-3. Ch 3, turn. Complete as for first side.

LEFT FRONT

With larger hook, ch 65 (73, 81, 89). Beg Lacy Squares Patt, and work even until piece measures approx 11½" from beg, ending after Row 2 of patt. Ch 4, turn.

Next Row (WS): Skip first dc, *dc into next ch-4 sp, ch 1, dc into next st, ch 1. Repeat from * across, ending row with dc under turning-ch-7, ch 1, dc into third ch of turning-ch-7—57 (65, 73, 81) sts. Ch 3, turn.

Next Row: Work as for Row 1 of Striped Lace Patt. Ch 4, turn.

Shape Armhole: Next Row (WS): Same as Row 2 of Striped Lace Patt leaving last 22 (26, 30, 36) sts unworked. Ch 3, turn.

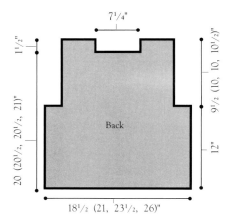

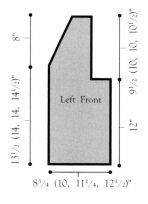

Note: These measurements do not include the edging.

Cont even in Striped Lace Patt until piece measures approx 13½ (14, 14, 14½)" from beg, ending after WS row.

Shape Neck: Dec Row 1 (RS): Dc into each st across until 3 sts rem in row, ending row with skip next dc, dec dc into turning-ch. Ch 4, turn.

Dec Row 2: Skip first 2 sts, *dc into next dc, ch 1, skip next dc. Repeat from * across row, ending row with dc into top of turning-ch-3. Ch 3, turn.

Repeat Dec Rows 1 and 2 six (six, seven, six) *more* times.

Work two rows even. Work Dec Rows 1 and 2. Repeat last four rows two (two, one, two) *more* times. Cont even until piece measures same as back. Fasten off.

RIGHT FRONT
Same as Left Front until piece measures approx 11½" from beg, ending after Row 2 of patt. Ch 4, turn.

Next Row (WS): Skip first dc, *dc into next ch-4 sp, ch 1, dc into next st, ch 1. Repeat from * across, ending row with dc under turning-ch-7, ch 1, dc into third ch of turning-ch-7—57 (65, 73, 81) sts. Ch 3, turn.

Next Row: Work same as Row 1 of Striped Lace Patt. *Do not ch 4 to turn.*

Shape Armhole: Next Row (WS): Slip st into first 23 (27, 31, 37) sts, ch 4, *skip next dc, dc into next dc, ch 1. Repeat from * across, ending row with dc into top of turning-ch-3—35 (39, 43, 45) sts. Ch 3, turn.

Cont even in Striped Lace Patt until piece measures approx 13½ (14, 14, 14½)" from beg, ending after WS row.

Shape Neck: Dec Row 1 (RS): Skip first dc, dc into next ch-1 sp, skip next dc, dc into each st across, ending row with dc under turning-ch-4, dc into third ch of turning-ch-4. Ch 4, turn.

Dec Row 2: Skip first 2 sts, *dc into next dc, ch 1, skip next dc. Repeat from * across, ending row with skip last 2 dc, dc into top of turning-ch-3. Ch 3, turn.

Repeat Dec Rows 1 and 2 six (six, seven, six) *more* times.

Work two rows even. Work Dec Rows 1 and 2. Repeat last four rows two (two, one, two) *more* times. Complete as for left front.

FINISHING
Lower Back Edging: With RS facing and larger hook, attach yarn with a slip st to first dc and ch 1.

Row 1 (RS): Working along opposite side of foundation ch, sc into same st as slip st, *2 sc into next ch-sp, sc into next dc, 2 sc into next ch-sp, sc into next sc. Repeat from * across, ending row with 3 sc under turning-ch. Ch 1, turn.

Row 2: Sc into first sc, *ch 2, skip next 2 sc, sc into next sc. Repeat from * across. Ch 1, turn.

Row 3: Sc into first sc, *ch 6, slip st into fourth ch from hook, 3 dc into same sc as last sc, skip next ch-2 sp, sc into next sc. Repeat from * across. Fasten off.

Front Lower Borders: With RS facing and larger hook, attach yarn with a slip st to first sc and ch 1. Complete as for back lower edging.

Sew shoulder seams. Sew side seams.

Front Bands: With RS facing and smaller hook, attach yarn with a slip st to lower right front edge and ch 1. Work rows of sc along right front edge, around neckline, and down left front edge until band measures ¾" from beg, working 2 sc at beg of each front neck shaping and working dec sc at beg of each back of neck shaping on RS rows. Place markers for six evenly-spaced buttons along left front, making the first ½" from bottom edge and the last ¼" from beg of front neck shaping. **Next Row:** Cont in sc as before, and make six buttonholes along right front by working (ch 4, skip next 4 sc) opposite markers. **Next Row:** Cont in sc as before, and work 4 sc into each ch-4 sp. Cont in sc as before until band measures 1½" from beg. Fasten off.

Armhole Edging: With RS facing and smaller hook, attach yarn with a slip st to beg of armhole shaping and ch 1. Work four rnds of sc around armhole, working a dec sc at beg of armhole shaping, top of side seam and at shoulder seam. Fasten off.

Sew on buttons.

Girl's Summer Top

INTERMEDIATE SKILL LEVEL

SIZES

Girl's size 8 (10, 12, 14). Instructions are for smallest size, with changes for other sizes noted in parentheses as necessary.

FINISHED MEASUREMENTS

Chest: 26 (28, 29, 31)"
Length (Excluding shoulder straps and lower edging): 9 (9½, 10, 10½)"

MATERIALS

Coats and Clark's *Lustersheen* (fingering weight, 100% acrylic; 1⅘ oz; approx 150 yds), 4 (5, 5, 6) balls Serenity #30
Crochet hook, sizes D/3 and E/4 or size needed to obtain gauge
Two ½" buttons (JHB International's *Linda Style #36364* was used on sample garment)

GAUGE

With larger hook, in Solid Shell Patt, 25 sts and 14 rows = 4".
To measure your gauge, make a test swatch as follows: With larger hook, ch 26.
Work Solid Shell Patt for fourteen rows total. Fasten off.
Piece should measure 4" square. **To save time, take time to check gauge.**

NOTE

Each sc, dc and turning-ch-3 counts as one st.

SOLID SHELL PATT

(Ch mult. 6 + 2)
Foundation Row (RS): Sc into second ch from hook, *skip next 2 ch, 5 dc into next ch, skip next 2 ch, sc into next ch. Repeat from * across. Ch 3, turn.
Row 1 (WS): 2 Dc into first sc, *skip next 2 dc, sc into next dc, skip next 2 dc, 5 dc into next sc. Repeat from * across, ending row with skip next 2 dc, sc into next dc, skip next 2 dc, 3 dc into last sc. Ch 1, turn.
Row 2: Sc into first dc, *skip next 2 dc, 5 dc into next sc, skip next 2 dc, sc into next dc. Repeat from * across, ending row with skip next 2 dc, 5 dc into next sc, skip next 2 dc, sc into top of turning-ch-3. Ch 3, turn.
Repeat Rows 1 and 2 for patt.

BACK

With larger hook, ch 80 (86, 92, 98). Beg Solid Shell Patt, and work even on 79 (85, 91, 97) sts until piece measures approx 6½ (6¾, 7, 7¼)" from beg, ending after Row 2 of patt. Fasten off.

FRONT

Work same as back until piece measures approx 6½ (6¾, 7, 7¼)" from beg, ending after Row 2 of patt. *Do not ch to turn.*

Shape Armholes: Next Row: Slip st into first 4 sts, ch 1, sc into same dc as last slip st, *skip next 2 dc, 5 dc into next sc, skip next 2 dc, sc into next dc. Repeat from * across until 3 sts rem in row, turn, leaving rest of row unworked—73 (79, 85, 91) sts. *Do not ch to turn.*

Dec Row: Slip st into first sc and into next 3 dc, ch 1, sc into same dc as last slip st, *skip next 2 dc, 5 dc into next sc, skip next 2 dc, sc into next dc. Repeat from * across until 3 sts rem in row, turn, leaving rest of row unworked. *Do not ch to turn.*

Repeat Dec Row two *more* times—55 (61, 67, 73) sts rem. Cont even in patt as established until piece measures approx 9 (9½, 10, 10½)" from beg, ending after RS row. *Do not ch to turn.*

Shoulder Strap for Left Side: Next Row (WS): Slip st into first 4 sts, change to smaller hook, ch 3, (4 dc, ch 3, slip st) into same dc as last slip st, ch 3, turn.

Next Row: (4 Dc, ch 3, slip st) into ch-3 sp just made, ch 3, turn.

Repeat last row until strap measures approx 11 (12, 13, 14)" from beg or until desired length. Fasten off.

Shoulder Strap for Right Side: With WS facing and smaller hook, attach yarn with a slip st to middle dc of last 5-dc group on other side of front. Ch 3, (4 dc, ch 3, slip st) into same dc as last slip st, ch 3, turn. Complete as for first strap.

FINISHING

Lower Back Edging: With RS facing and smaller hook, attach yarn with a slip st to first sc and ch 1.

Row 1 (RS): Working along opposite side of foundation ch, sc into same st as slip st, *ch 3, skip next 2 sts, sc into next st. Repeat from * across. Ch 4, turn.

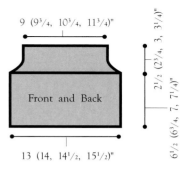

9 (9³/₄, 10³/₄, 11³/₄)"

Front and Back

2¹/₂ (2³/₄, 3, 3¹/₄)"

6¹/₂ (6³/₄, 7, 7¹/₄)"

13 (14, 14¹/₂, 15¹/₂)"

Note: These measurements do
not include the edging.

Row 2: *Sc into next ch-3 sp, ch 3. Repeat from * across, ending row with sc into next ch-3 sp, ch 1, dc into last sc. Ch 1, turn.

Row 3: Sc into first dc, *8 dc into next ch-3 sp, sc into next ch-3 sp. Repeat from * across, ending row with 8 dc into next ch-3 sp, sc under turning-ch-4. Fasten off.

Lower Front Edging: With RS facing and smaller hook, attach yarn with a slip st to first sc and ch 1. Complete as for back lower edging.

Front Armhole Edging for Left Side: With RS facing and larger hook, attach yarn with a slip st to beg of armhole shaping and ch 1. Work one row of sc along armhole shaping, ending with a slip st to sc before shoulder strap. Fasten off.

Front Armhole Edging for Right Side: With RS facing and larger hook, attach yarn with a slip st to sc next to shoulder strap at armhole edge and ch 1. Work one row of sc along armhole shaping, ending with a slip st to last st. Fasten off.

Sew side seams. Sew buttons onto WS of back opposite shoulder straps. To button the adjustable straps, use one of the vertical ch-3 spaces as a buttonhole to achieve the best strap length.

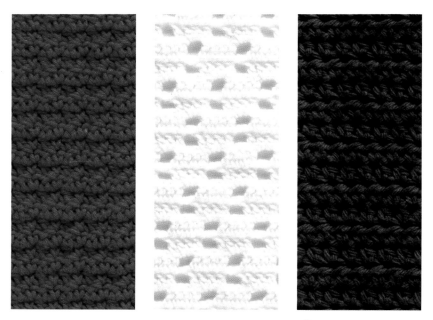

all-american threesome

This casual ensemble is perfect for cool spring and summer evenings. And the patriotic colors will enliven everyone's wardrobe!

Man's Zippered Jacket

INTERMEDIATE SKILL LEVEL

SIZES

Man's Small (Medium, Large, Extra-Large). Instructions are for smallest size, with changes for other sizes noted in parentheses as necessary.

FINISHED MEASUREMENTS

Chest (Zipped): 45½ (50, 53½, 58)"
Length: 25½ (25½, 27½, 27½)"
Sleeve width at underarm: 19 (19¾, 21, 21¾)"

MATERIALS

Spinrite/Lily's *Sugar 'n Cream Sport* (sport weight, 100% cotton; 1¾ oz; approx 125 yds), 24 (25, 27, 28) skeins Red #14
Crochet hooks, sizes E/4 and F/5 or size needed to obtain gauge
18 (18, 20, 20)" separating zipper (Coats and Clark's *Separating Sport Zipper, Art. F.43*, was used on sample garment)

GAUGE

In Textured Patt with larger hook, 20 sts and 14 rows = 4".
To measure your gauge, make a test swatch as follows: Ch 22.
Foundation Row: Sc into third ch from hook, *dc into next ch, sc into next ch. Repeat from * across, ending row with hdc into last ch—20 sts plus turning-ch. Ch 2, turn.
Next Row: Work Patt Row of Textured Patt. Ch 2, turn.
Repeat last row thirteen *more* times. Fasten off.
Piece should measure 4¼" square. **To save time, take time to check gauge.**

NOTES

To decrease, work a dec hdc to combine the first 2 sts and/or the last 2 sts of the row.
Dec hdc = (Yarn over, insert hook into next st and pull up a loop) twice, yarn over and draw it through all five loops on hook.
To increase, work 2 sts into one st. Each hdc, sc, dc, turning-ch-2, and turning-ch-3 counts as one st.

RIB PATT

(Over an odd number of ch)
Foundation Row (RS): Dc into fourth ch from hook and into each ch across. Ch 2, turn.
Row 1 (WS): Skip first st, *FPDC into next st, BPDC into next st. Repeat from * across, ending row with FPDC into next st, hdc into top of turning-ch. Ch 2, turn.
Row 2: Skip first st, *BPDC into next st, FPDC into next st. Repeat from * across, ending row with BPDC into next st, hdc into top of turning-ch-2. Ch 2, turn.
Repeat Rows 1 and 2 for patt.

TEXTURED PATT

(Mult. 2 + 1 sts)
Foundation Row (WS): Skip first st, *sc into next st, dc into next st. Repeat from * across, ending row with sc into next st, hdc into top of turning-ch-2. Ch 2, turn.
Patt Row: Skip first hdc, *sc into next sc, dc into next dc. Repeat from * across, ending row with sc into next sc, hdc into top of turning-ch-2. Ch 2, turn.
Repeat Patt Row.

BACK

With larger hook, ch 113 (123, 133, 143). Work Rib Patt on 111 (121, 131, 141) sts for three rows. Beg Textured Patt, and work even until piece measures approx 16 (15½, 17, 16½)" from beg, ending after WS row.

Shape Armholes: Next Row (RS): Dec 1 st each side.

Repeat last row five *more* times—99 (109, 119, 129) sts rem.

Work even until piece measures approx 25½ (25½, 27½, 27½)" from beg. Fasten off.

POCKET LININGS
(Make Two)
With larger hook, ch 28.

Foundation Row: Sc into second ch from hook and into each ch across—27 sc. Ch 1, turn.

Next Row: Sc into each sc across. Ch 1, turn.

Repeat last row until piece measures approx 5" from beg. Fasten off.

RIGHT FRONT

With larger hook, ch 57 (63, 67, 73). Work Rib Patt on 55 (61, 65, 71) sts for three rows. Beg Textured Patt, and work even until piece measures approx 6" from beg, ending after WS row.

Place Pocket Lining: Next Row (RS): Work patt across first 14 (17, 19, 22) sts, cont in Textured Patt across 27 sts of one pocket lining, skip next 27 sts of right front, work to end row.

Cont even until piece measures same as back to armholes, ending after RS row.

Shape Armhole: Next Row (WS): Cont in patt as established, and dec 1 st at beg of next row. Dec 1 st at armhole edge every row five *more* times—49 (55, 59, 65) sts rem.

Cont even until piece measures 18 (18, 20, 20)" from beg, ending after WS row.

Shape Neck: Cont in patt as established, and dec 1 st at neck edge every row 14 (17, 14, 17) times, then every other row 4 (3, 4, 3) times—31 (35, 41, 45) sts rem. Cont even until piece measures same as back. Fasten off.

LEFT FRONT
Work same as left front, *except* reverse all shaping.

SLEEVES
With larger hook, ch 47 (47, 51, 51). Work Rib Patt on 45 (45, 49, 49) sts for three rows. Beg Textured Patt, and inc 1 st each side every row 0 (0, 0, 2) times, then every other row 20 (24, 27, 28) times, then every fourth row 5 (3, 1, 0) times—95 (99, 105, 109) sts—working new sts into Textured Patt. Cont even until piece measures approx 19¹⁄₂ (19¹⁄₂, 19, 19)" from beg, ending after WS row.

Shape Cap: Next Row (RS): Cont in patt as established, and dec 1 st each side every row five times—85 (89, 95, 99) sts rem. Fasten off.

FINISHING
Sew shoulder seams.

Front and Neck Edging: With RS facing and smaller hook, attach yarn with a slip st to lower right front edge and ch 1.

Row 1 (RS): Sc evenly along right front edge, around back of neck, and down left front edge, working 2 sc at beg of front neck shaping on both sides and working a dec sc at each shoulder seam. Ch 1, turn.

Row 2 (WS): Work another row of sc along left front edge, around back of neck and down right front, working increases and decreases as before. Fasten off.

Pocket Bands: With RS facing and smaller hook, attach yarn with a slip st to top of pocket edge and ch 1. Work 26 sc along top of pocket. Ch 1, turn.

Next Row: Sc into each sc. Ch 1, turn.

Repeat last row one *more* time. Fasten off.

Sew sides of pocket band to front. Sew pocket linings to WS of front.

Set in sleeves. Sew sleeve and side seams. Sew in zipper.

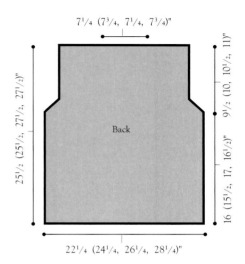

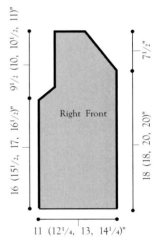

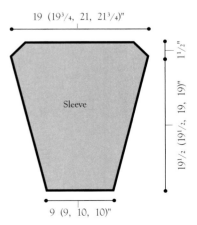

Woman's White Cardigan

INTERMEDIATE SKILL LEVEL

SIZES

Woman's Petite (Small, Medium, Large, Extra-Large). Instructions are for smallest size, with changes for other sizes noted in parentheses as necessary.

FINISHED MEASUREMENTS

Bust (Buttoned): $37^{1}/_{2}$ ($41^{1}/_{4}$, 45, $48^{1}/_{4}$, $51^{1}/_{2}$)"
Length (Before edging): $21^{1}/_{2}$ ($21^{1}/_{2}$, $23^{3}/_{4}$, $23^{3}/_{4}$, 25)"
Sleeve width at underarm: 18 (18, 19, 19, 20)"

MATERIALS

Coats and Clark's *Lustersheen* (fingering weight, 100% acrylic; $1^{4}/_{5}$ oz; approx 150 yds), 13 (14, 15, 16, 17) balls White #001
Crochet hook, sizes C/2 and E/4 or size needed to obtain gauge
Six $^{3}/_{4}$" buttons (JHB International's *Hartford Style #49795* was used on sample garment)

GAUGE

With larger hook, in Checkerboard Lace Patt, 28 sts and 13 rows = 4".
To measure your gauge, make a test swatch as follows: With larger hook, ch 30.
Work Checkerboard Lace Patt for thirteen rows total. Fasten off.
Piece should measure 4" square. **To save time, take time to check gauge.**

NOTES

Each dc and turning-ch-3 counts as one st; each ch-2 sp counts as 2 sts; each turning-ch-5 counts as 3 sts (one dc plus one ch-2 sp).
3-dc cluster = (Yarn over, insert hook into indicated ch-2 sp and pull up a loop, yarn over and draw it through two loops) three times, yarn over and draw it through all four loops on hook.

CHECKERBOARD LACE PATT

(Ch mult. 6)
Foundation Row (RS): Dc into fourth ch from hook and into next 2 ch, *ch 2, skip next 2 ch, dc into next 4 ch. Repeat from * across. Ch 3, turn.
Row 1 (WS): Skip first dc, dc into next 3 dc, *ch 2, skip next ch-2 sp, dc into next 4 dc. Repeat from * across, ending row with ch 2, skip next ch-2 sp, dc into next 3 dc, dc into top of turning-ch-3. Ch 5, turn.
Row 2: Skip first 3 dc, *dc into next dc, 2 dc into next ch-2 sp, dc into next dc, ch 2, skip next 2 dc. Repeat from * across, ending row with dc into top of turning-ch-3. Ch 5, turn.
Row 3: Skip first dc and ch-2 sp, *dc into next 4 dc, ch 2, skip next ch-2 sp. Repeat from * across, ending row with dc into next 4 dc, ch 2, dc into third ch of turning-ch-5. Ch 3, turn.
Row 4: Skip first dc, *2 dc into next ch-2 sp, dc into next dc, ch 2, skip next 2 dc, dc into next dc. Repeat from * across, ending row with 2 dc under turning-ch-5, dc into third ch of turning-ch-5. Ch 3, turn.
Repeat Rows 1-4 for patt.

BACK

With larger hook, ch 132 (144, 156, 168, 180). Beg Checkerboard Lace Patt, working even on 130 (142, 154, 166, 178) sts until piece measures approx $12^{1}/_{2}$ ($12^{1}/_{2}$, $14^{1}/_{4}$, $14^{1}/_{4}$, 15)" from beg, ending after Row 3 of patt. *Do not ch 3 to turn.*

Shape Armholes: Next Row (RS): Slip st into first 13 (13, 19, 19, 25) sts, ch 3, cont in patt as established across row until 12 (12, 18, 18, 24) sts rem in row, leaving rest of row unworked—106 (118, 118, 130, 130) sts. Ch 3, turn.

Work even until piece measures approx $20^{1}/_{2}$ ($20^{1}/_{2}$, $22^{3}/_{4}$, $22^{3}/_{4}$, 24)" from beg, ending after Row 3 of patt. Ch 3, turn.

Shape Neck: Work across first 28 (34, 34, 40, 40) sts, ch 3, turn, leaving rest of row unworked. Cont even on this side for two more rows, until piece measures approx $21^{1}/_{2}$ ($21^{1}/_{2}$, $23^{3}/_{4}$, $23^{3}/_{4}$, 25)" from beg. Fasten off.

For second side of neck, with RS facing, skip the middle 50 sts, attach yarn with a slip st to next st and ch 5. Complete same as first side.

RIGHT FRONT

With larger hook, ch 66 (72, 78, 84, 90). Beg Checkerboard Lace Patt, and work even on 64 (70, 76, 82, 88) sts until piece measures approx $12^{1}/_{2}$ ($12^{1}/_{2}$, $14^{1}/_{4}$, $14^{1}/_{4}$, 15)" from beg, ending after Row 3 of patt. Ch 3, turn.

Shape Armhole: Next Row (RS): Cont in patt as established across first 52 (58, 58, 64, 64) sts, ch 3, turn, leaving last 12 (12, 18, 18, 24) sts unworked.

Cont even in patt as established until piece measures approx 13½ (13½, 14¾, 14¾, 16)" from beg, ending after Row 3 of patt. Ch 3, turn.

Neck Dec Row 1 (RS): Skip first dc and ch-2 sp, dc into next dc, work patt as established to end row. Ch 3, turn.

Neck Dec Row 2: Work patt as established across, ending row with ch 2, skip next ch-2 sp, skip next dc, dc into top of turning-ch-3. Ch 3, turn.

Repeat Neck Dec Rows 1 and 2 seven *more* times—28 (34, 34, 40, 40) sts rem. Cont even until piece measures same as back. Fasten off.

LEFT FRONT
Work same as right front until piece measures same as back to armhole, ending after Row 3 of patt. *Do not ch 3 to turn.*

Shape Armhole: Next Row (RS): Slip st into first 13 (13, 19, 19, 25) sts, ch 3, cont in patt to end row.

Work even in patt as established until piece measures approx 13½ (13½, 14¾, 14¾, 16)" from beg, ending after Row 3 of patt. Ch 3, turn.

Shape Neck: Neck Dec Row 1 (RS): Work patt as established until 6 sts rem in row, ending row with ch 2, skip next 2 dc, dc into last dc, dc into third ch of turning-ch-5. Ch 5, turn.

Neck Dec Row 2: Skip first 2 dc and ch-2 sp, dc into next 4 dc, work patt as established to end row.

Repeat Neck Dec Rows 1 and 2 seven *more* times—28 (34, 34, 40, 40) sts rem. Complete same as back. Fasten off.

SLEEVES
With larger hook, ch 66 (66, 72, 72, 78). Work two rows of Checkerboard Lace Patt—64 (64, 70, 70, 76) sts each row. Ch 3, turn.

Sleeve Inc Row 1 (RS): Dc into first dc, *ch 2, skip next 2 dc, dc into next dc, 2 dc into next ch-2 sp, dc into next dc. Repeat from * across, ending row with ch 2, 2 dc into top of turning-ch-3. Ch 3, turn.

Sleeve Inc Row 2: Dc into first dc, 2 dc into next dc, *ch 2, skip next ch-2 sp, dc into next 4 dc. Repeat from * across, ending row with ch 2, skip next ch-2 sp, 2 dc into next dc, 2 dc into top of turning-ch-3. Ch 3, turn.

Repeat Sleeve Inc Rows 1 and 2 twice *more*. Ch 5, turn.

Work four rows even in patt as established. Work Sleeve Inc Rows 1 and 2 once *more*.
Repeat last six rows six *more* times.

Next Row (RS): Work same as Sleeve Inc Row 1. Ch 3, turn.

Next Row: Dc into first dc, *ch 2, skip next ch-2 sp, dc into next 4 dc. Repeat from * across, ending row with ch 2, skip next ch-2 sp, dc into next dc, dc into top of turning-ch-3. Ch 3, turn.

Cont even in patt as established on 126 (126, 132, 132, 138) sts until piece measures approx 20½ (20¼, 20½, 19¾, 20)" from beg. Fasten off.

FINISHING

Lower Back Edging: With RS facing and smaller hook, attach yarn with a slip st to lower edge of back and ch 1.

Row 1 (RS): Work 130 (142, 154, 166, 178) sc into unused loops of foundation chain. Ch 1, turn.

Row 2: Sc into each sc across. Ch 1, turn.

Row 3: Work same as last row. Ch 5, turn.

Row 4: Skip first 3 sc, *dc into next sc, ch 2, skip next 2 sc. Repeat from * across, ending row with dc into last sc. Ch 1, turn.

Row 5: Sc into first dc, *ch 3, 3-dc cluster into next ch-2 sp, ch 3, slip st into third ch from hook, ch 3, sc into next dc, ch 3, sc into next dc. Repeat from * across, ending row with ch 3, 3-dc cluster under turning-ch, ch 3, slip st into third ch from hook, ch 3, sc into third ch of turning-ch-5. Fasten off.

Lower Right Front Edging: With RS facing and smaller hook, attach yarn with a slip st to lower edge of right front and ch 1.

Row 1 (RS): Work 64 (70, 76, 82, 88) sc into unused loops of foundation chain. Ch 1, turn.

Rows 2-5: Work same as lower back edging.

Lower Left Front Edging: Work same as lower right front edging.

Lower Sleeve Edging: With RS facing and smaller hook, attach yarn with a slip st to lower edge of sleeve and ch 1.

Row 1 (RS): Work 64 (64, 70, 70, 76) sc into unused loops of foundation chain. Ch 1, turn.

Rows 2-5: Work same as lower back edging.

Sew shoulder seams.

Front Bands: With RS facing and smaller hook, attach yarn with a slip st to front edge of right front and ch 1. Work rows of sc along right front, around back of neck, and down left front until band measures approx ½" from beg, inc 1 sc at beg of front neck shaping each side every row and dec 1 sc at beg of back neck shaping each side every row. Place markers for six evenly-spaced buttonholes along right front, making the first one ½" from lower edge and the last one ¼" from beg of neck shaping.

Next Row: Make six buttonholes by working (ch 4, skip next 4 sc) where marked.

Next Row: Cont in sc, working 4 sc into each ch-4 sp of the previous row.

Cont even until band measures approx 1" from beg. Fasten off.

Set in sleeves. Sew sleeve and side seams. Sew on buttons.

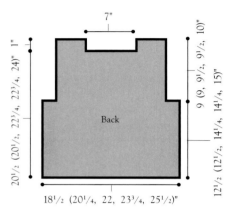

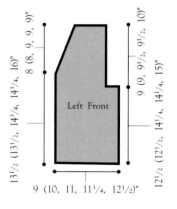

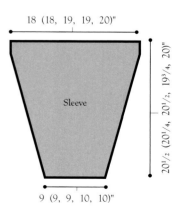

Child's Patriotic Pullover

INTERMEDIATE SKILL LEVEL

SIZES
Child's size 2 (4, 6, 8). Instructions are for smallest size, with changes for other sizes noted in parentheses as necessary.

FINISHED MEASUREMENTS
Chest: 26 (30, 32, 34)"
Length: 15 (16, 17$\frac{1}{2}$, 18$\frac{3}{4}$)"
Sleeve width at underarm: 13 (13$\frac{1}{2}$, 14$\frac{1}{2}$, 16)"

MATERIALS
Elmore-Pisgah's *Peaches & Creme* (worsted weight, 100% cotton; 2.5 oz; approx 122 yds), 2 (3, 4, 4) skeins Red #95 (A), 5 (6, 6, 7) skeins Deep Purple #49 (B), 1 (2, 2, 3) skeins White #1 (C), and 1 (1, 2, 2) skeins Yellow #10 (D)
Crochet hooks, sizes G/6 and H/8 or size needed to obtain gauge

GAUGE
With larger hook, 16 hdc and 12 rows = 4".
To measure your gauge, make a test swatch as follows: With larger hook and A, ch 17.
Foundation Row: Hdc into third ch from hook and into each ch across—16 hdc. Ch 2, turn.
Next Row: Skip first hdc, hdc into each hdc across, ending row with hdc into top of turning-ch-2. Ch 2, turn.
Repeat last row ten *more* times. Fasten off.
Piece should measure 4" square. **To save time, take time to check gauge.**

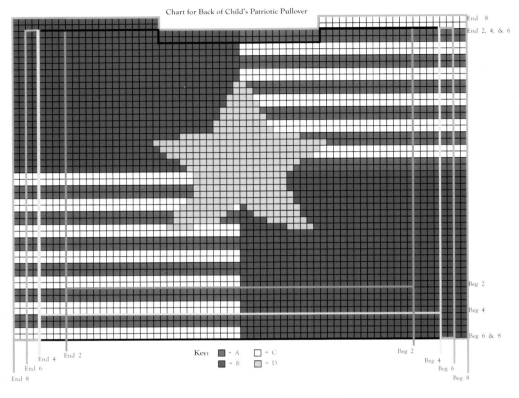

Chart for Back of Child's Patriotic Pullover

Key: ■ = A □ = C
■ = B ▨ = D

NOTES

Each turning-ch-2 counts as one hdc.
To decrease, work a dec hdc to combine the first 2 sts and/or the last 2 sts of the row.
Dec hdc = (Yarn over, insert hook into next st and pull up a loop) twice, yarn over and draw it through all five loops on hook.
To increase, work 2 sts into one st.
To change color, work until 3 loops rem on hook; with the new color, complete the st; fasten off the old color.

RIB PATT

(Over an even number of ch)
Foundation Row (RS): Dc into fourth ch from hook and into each ch across. Ch 2, turn.
Row 1 (WS): Skip first st, *FPDC into next st, BPDC into next st. Repeat from * across, ending row with hdc into top of turning-ch. Ch 2, turn.
Row 2: Skip first st, *FPDC into next st, BPDC into next st. Repeat from * across, ending row with hdc into top of turning-ch-2. Ch 2, turn.
Repeat Rows 1 and 2 for patt.

PATRIOTIC CHART FOR FRONT AND BACK

See charts.

BACK

With smaller hook and A, ch 54 (62, 66, 70). Work Rib Patt until piece measures approx 1½ (1½, 1½, 2)" from beg, ending after WS row—52 (60, 64, 68) sts each row. Change to larger hook and B. Ch 2, turn.

Next Row: Beg where indicated, work first row of Patriotic Chart in hdc. Ch 2, turn.

Follow chart, and cont even until Row 38 (42, 46, 48) of Patriotic Chart is completed. Ch 2, turn.

Shape Neck: Next Row (RS): Skip first hdc, work across next 13 (17, 19, 21) hdc, ch 2, turn, leaving rest of row unworked.

Follow chart, and cont even for one more row. Fasten off.

For second side of neck, with RS facing, skip the middle 24 hdc, attach B with a slip st to next hdc and ch 2. Work hdc into next 12 (16, 18, 20) hdc, hdc into top of turning-ch-2.

Follow chart, and cont even for one more row. Fasten off.

FRONT

Work as for back until Row 34 (38, 42, 42) of Patriotic Chart is completed. Ch 2, turn.

Shape Neck: Next Row (RS): Skip first hdc, hdc into next 17 (21, 23, 25) dc. Turn, leaving rest of row unworked. *Do not ch 2 to turn.*

Next Row: Slip st into first 4 hdc, ch 2, hdc into next 13 (17, 19, 21) hdc, hdc into top of turning-ch-2. Ch 2, turn.

Next Row: Skip first hdc, hdc into next 12 (16, 18, 20) hdc, work a dec hdc to combine the next hdc and turning-ch-2— 14 (18, 20, 22) sts rem. Cont even until chart is completed. Fasten off.

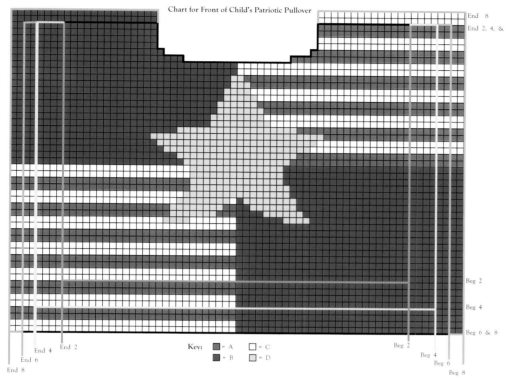

Chart for Front of Child's Patriotic Pullover

End 8
End 2, 4, & 6

Beg 2
Beg 4
Beg 6 & 8

End 4   End 2
End 6
End 8

Key: ■ = A   □ = C
      ■ = B   ▨ = D

Beg 2
Beg 4
Beg 6
Beg 8

Rnd 2: Skip first st, *FPDC into next st, BPDC into next st. Repeat from * around, ending rnd with FPDC, slip st to top of ch-2. Ch 2.

Repeat last rnd once (once, twice, twice) *more*. Fasten off.

Place markers 6½ (6¾, 7¼, 8)" down from shoulders. Set in sleeves between markers. Sew sleeve and side seams.

For second side of neck, with RS facing, skip the middle 16 hdc, attach B with a slip st to next hdc and ch 2. Work hdc into next 16 (20, 22, 24) hdc, hdc into top of turning-ch-2. Ch 2, turn.

Next Row (WS): Skip first hdc, hdc into next 14 (18, 20, 22) hdc. Ch 2, turn, leaving rest of row unworked.

Next Row: Skip first hdc, work a dec hdc to combine the next 2 hdc, hdc into next 11 (15, 17, 19) hdc, hdc into top of turning-ch-2. Ch 2, turn. Complete as for first side.

SLEEVES

With smaller hook and A, ch 30 (30, 30, 32). Work Rib Patt until piece measures approx 1½ (1½, 1½, 2)" from beg, ending after WS row—28 (28, 28, 30) sts each row. Change to larger hook and B. Ch 2, turn.

Next Row (RS): Skip first st, hdc into each st across, ending row with hdc into top of turning-ch-2. Ch 2, turn.

Repeat last row, and inc 1 st each side every other row 11 (11, 13, 17) times, then every fourth row 1 (2, 2, 0) times—52 (54, 58, 64) sts. Cont even until sleeve measures approx 10¾ (12½, 13½, 14)" from beg. Fasten off.

FINISHING
Sew shoulder seams.

Neckband: With RS facing and smaller hook, attach A with a slip st to neck edge of right shoulder seam and ch 3.

Rnd 1: Work 62 (62, 62, 68) dc evenly around neckline. Slip st into top of ch-3. Ch 2, do not turn.

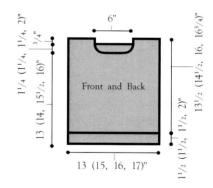

6"
1¼ (1¼, 1¼, 2)"
¾"
13 (14, 15½, 16)"
13½ (14½, 16, 16¾)"
1½ (1½, 1½, 2)"
Front and Back
13 (15, 16, 17)"

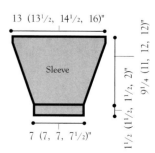

13 (13½, 14½, 16)"
9¼ (11, 12, 12)"
Sleeve
1½ (1½, 1½, 2)"
7 (7, 7, 7½)"

summer sunshine

Summertime feels happier and brighter with this great group for the girls!

Woman's Summertime T-shirt

INTERMEDIATE SKILL LEVEL

SIZES
Woman's Small (Medium, Large, Extra-Large). Instructions are for smallest size, with changes for other sizes noted in parentheses as necessary.

FINISHED MEASUREMENTS
Bust: 36 (40, 44, 48$\frac{1}{2}$)"
Length (Before edging): 19 (20, 21, 22)"
Sleeve width at underarm: 17 (18, 18$\frac{1}{2}$, 20)"

MATERIALS
Coats and Clark's *Lustersheen* (fingering weight, 100% acrylic; 1$\frac{4}{5}$ oz; approx 150 yds), 8 (9, 10, 11) balls Buttercup #227 (A) and 2 (3, 3, 4) balls White #001 (B)
Crochet hook, sizes C/2 and E/4 or size needed to obtain gauge

GAUGE
With larger hook, in solid sc, 23 sts and 24 rows = 4".
To measure your gauge, make a test swatch as follows: With larger hook, ch 24.
Foundation Row: Sc into second ch from hook and into each ch across—23 sc. Ch 1, turn.
Next Row: Sc into each sc across. Ch 1, turn.
Repeat last row twenty-two *more* times. Fasten off.
Piece should measure 4" square. **To save time, take time to check gauge.**

NOTES
5-dc dec = Holding back last loop, work dc into next 5 sts, yarn over and draw it through all six loops on hook.
Dec sc = (Insert hook into next st and pull up a loop) twice, yarn over and draw it through all three loops on hook.
To decrease, work a dec sc to combine the first 2 sts and/or the last 2 sts of the row.
To change color, work until two loops rem on hook; with second color, complete the st; fasten off first color.
To increase, work two sc into one sc.

ZIG-ZAG PATT
(Ch mult. 6 + 4)
Foundation Row (WS): 2 Dc into fourth ch from hook, *skip next 2 ch, sc into next ch, skip next 2 ch, 5 dc into next ch. Repeat from * across, ending row with skip next 2 ch, sc into next ch, skip next 2 ch, 3 dc into last ch. Change color, ch 1, turn.
Row 1 (RS): Sc into first dc, *ch 3, 5-dc dec to combine the next 5 sts, ch 3, sc into next dc. Repeat from * across, ending row with ch 3, 5-dc dec to combine the next 5 sts, ch 3, sc into top of turning-ch-3. Ch 3, turn.
Row 2: 2 Dc into first sc, *sc into next 5-dc dec, 5 dc into next sc. Repeat from * across, ending row with sc into next 5-dc dec, 3 dc into last sc. Change color, ch 1, turn.
Repeat Rows 1 and 2 in Stripe Patt.

STRIPE PATT
One row A, *two rows B, two rows A. Repeat from * for patt.

BACK
With larger hook and A, ch 106 (118, 130, 142). Beg Zig-Zag Patt, and work even until piece measures approx 7 (8, 8$\frac{1}{2}$, 9$\frac{1}{2}$)" from beg, ending after working a RS row worked with A. Ch 1, turn.

Next Row (WS): Sc into first sc, *2 sc into next ch-3 sp, sc into next 5-dc dec, 2 sc into next ch-3 sp, sc into next sc. Repeat from * across—103 (115, 127, 139) sc. Ch 1, turn.

Next Row: Sc into each sc across. Ch 1, turn.

Cont even in sc with A until piece measures approx 10$\frac{1}{2}$ (11, 11$\frac{3}{4}$, 12)" from beg, ending after WS row. Ch 1, turn.

Shape Armholes: Next Row (RS): Dec sc to combine the first 2 sts, sc across until 2 sts rem in row, ending row with dec sc to combine the last 2 sts. Ch 1, turn.

Repeat last row nine *more* times—83 (95, 107, 119) sts rem.

Next Row: Sc into each sc across. Ch 1, turn.

Cont even until piece measures approx 17 (18, 19, 20)" from beg, ending after WS row.

Shape Neck: Next Row (RS): Sc into first 25 (31, 37, 43) sc, ch 1, turn, leaving rest of row unworked.

Next Row: Dec sc to combine the first 2 sts, sc across to end row. Ch 1, turn.

Next Row: Sc across until 2 sts rem, ending row with dec sc to combine last 2 sts. Ch 2, turn.

Repeat last two rows once *more*. Cont even on 21 (27, 33, 39) sts until piece measures 19 (20, 21, 22)" from beg. Fasten off.

For second side of neck, with RS facing, skip the middle 33 sc, attach yarn with a slip st to next st and ch 1. Work to end row. Ch 1, turn.

Next Row (WS): Sc across until 2 sts rem, ending row with dec sc to combine last 2 sts. Ch 2, turn.

Next Row: Dec sc to combine the first 2 sts, sc across to end row. Ch 1, turn.

Repeat last two rows once *more*. Complete same as first side.

FRONT

Work same as back until piece measures approx 14³/₄ (15³/₄, 16³/₄, 17³/₄)" from beg, ending after WS row. Ch 1, turn.

Shape Neck: Next Row (RS): Sc into first 33 (39, 45, 51) sc, ch 1, turn, leaving rest of row unworked.

Next Row: Dec sc to combine the first 2 sts, sc across to end row. Ch 1, turn.

Next Row: Sc across until 2 sts rem, ending row with dec sc to combine last 2 sts. Ch 2, turn.

Repeat last two rows twice *more*.

Next Row (WS): Dec sc to combine the first 2 sts, sc across to end row. Ch 1, turn.

Next Row: Sc into each sc across. Ch 1, turn.

Repeat last two rows five *more* times—21 (27, 33, 39) sts rem.

Cont even until this side measures same as back to shoulder. Fasten off.

For second side of neck, with RS facing, skip the middle 17 sc, attach yarn with a slip st to next st and ch 1. Work to end row. Ch 1, turn.

Next Row (WS): Sc across until 2 sts rem, ending row with dec sc to combine last 2 sts. Ch 2, turn.

Next Row: Dec sc to combine the first 2 sts, sc across to end row. Ch 1, turn.

Repeat last two rows twice *more.*

Next Row (WS): Sc across until 2 sts rem, ending row with dec sc to combine last 2 sts. Ch 1, turn.

Next Row: Sc into each sc across. Ch 1, turn.

Repeat last two rows five *more* times—21 (27, 33, 39) sts rem. Complete same as first side.

SLEEVES

With larger hook and A, ch 76 (76, 82, 94). Work four rows of Zig-Zag Patt in Stripe Patt. Ch 1, turn.

Next Row (WS): Sc into first sc, *2 sc into next ch-3 sp, sc into next 5-dc dec, 2 sc into next ch-3 sp, sc into next sc. Repeat from * across. Ch 1, turn—73 (73, 79, 91) sc.

Next Row: Sc into each sc across. Ch 1, turn.

Cont in sc with A, and inc 1 st each side every row 8 (14, 14, 12) times, then every other row 4 (1, 0, 0) times—97 (103, 107, 115) sts.

Cont even until piece measures approx 4¼" from beg, ending after WS row. Ch 1, turn.

Shape Cap: Next Row (RS): Dec sc to combine the first 2 sts, sc across until 2 sts rem in row, ending row with dec sc to combine the last 2 sts. Ch 1, turn.

Repeat last row nine *more* times—77 (83, 87, 95) sts rem. Fasten off.

FINISHING

Sew shoulder seams.

Neckband: With RS facing and smaller hook, join A with a slip st at neck edge of right shoulder seam and ch 1.

Rnd 1 (RS): Work 120 sc evenly around neckline. Join with a slip st to first sc. Ch 1, do not turn.

Rnd 2 (RS): Sc into same sc as last slip st, *skip next 2 sc, 5 dc into next sc, skip next 2 sc, sc into next sc. Repeat from * around, ending rnd with skip next 2 sc, 5 dc into next sc, skip next 2 sc, slip st to first sc. Fasten off.

Set in sleeves. Sew sleeve and side seams.

Bottom Border: With RS facing and smaller hook, attach A with a slip st to lower right side seam and ch 1.

Rnd 1 (RS): Working into unused loops of foundation ch, work 204 (228, 252, 276) sc around lower edge. Join with slip st to first sc. Ch 1, do not turn.

Rnd 2 (RS): Sc into same sc as last slip st, *skip next 2 sc, 5 dc into next sc, skip next 2 sc, sc into next sc. Repeat from * around, ending rnd with skip next 2 sc, 5 dc into next sc, skip next 2 sc, slip st to first sc. Fasten off.

Sleeve Border: With RS facing and smaller hook, attach A with a slip st to lower sleeve seam and ch 1.

Rnd 1 (RS): Working into unused loops of foundation ch, work 72 (72, 78, 90) sc around lower edge. Join with a slip st to first sc. Ch 1, do not turn.

Rnd 2 (RS): Sc into same sc as last slip st, *skip next 2 sc, 5 dc into next sc, skip next 2 sc, sc into next sc. Repeat from * around, ending rnd with skip next 2 sc, 5 dc into next sc, skip next 2 sc, slip st to first sc. Fasten off.

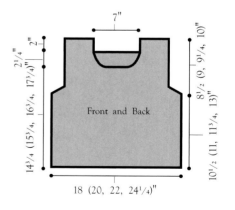

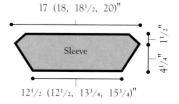

Girl's Dress

INTERMEDIATE SKILL LEVEL

SIZES
Child's size 2 (4, 6). Instructions are for smallest size, with changes for other sizes noted in parentheses as necessary.

FINISHED MEASUREMENTS
Chest: 20 (23, 25$\frac{1}{2}$)"
Length: 18$\frac{1}{2}$ (19$\frac{1}{4}$, 20$\frac{1}{2}$)"

MATERIALS
Coats and Clark's *Red Heart Baby Fingering* (fingering weight, 100% acrylic; 1$\frac{3}{4}$ oz; approx 270 yds), 1 (2, 2) skeins White #1 (A), 3 (3, 4) skeins Baby Yellow #224 (B), and 10 yds of Pastel Green #680 (C)
Crochet hooks, sizes C/2 and D/3 or size needed to obtain gauge
One (two, three) $\frac{1}{2}$" buttons (JHB International's *Moonstone Style # 71623* was used on sample garment)

GAUGE
With larger hook, 26 sc and 28 rows = 4".
To measure your gauge, make a test swatch as follows: With larger hook and A, ch 27.
Foundation Row: Sc into second ch from hook and into each ch across—26 sc. Ch 1, turn.
Next Row: Sc into each sc across. Ch 1, turn.
Repeat last row twenty-six *more* times. Fasten off.
Piece should measure 4" square. **To save time, take time to check gauge.**

NOTES
To decrease, work a dec sc to combine the first 2 sts and/or the last 2 sts of the row.
Dec sc = (Insert hook into next st and pull up a loop) twice, yarn over and draw it through all three loops on hook.
To increase, work 2 sts into one st.
2-dc cluster = (Yarn over, insert hook into indicated st and pull up a loop, yarn over and draw it through two loops) twice, yarn over and draw it through all three loops on hook.

BACK BODICE
With larger hook and A, ch 66 (75, 84).

Foundation Row (RS): Sc into second ch from hook and into each ch across—65 (74, 83) sc. Ch 1, turn.

Next Row: Sc into each sc across. Ch 1, turn.

Repeat last row until piece measures approx 3 (3$\frac{1}{4}$, 4)" from beg, ending after WS row. *Do not ch 1 to turn.*

Shape Armholes: Next Row (RS): Slip st into first 5 sc, ch 1, sc into same sc as slip st, sc into next 56 (65, 74) sc, ch 1, turn, leaving rest of row unworked—57 (66, 75) sts.

Dec 1 st each side every row four times, then dec 1 st each side every other row two (three, four) times—45 (52, 59) sts rem.

Cont even until piece measures approx 6$\frac{1}{2}$ (7$\frac{1}{4}$, 8$\frac{1}{2}$)" from beg, ending after WS row. Ch 1, turn.

Shape Neck: Next Row (RS): Work across first 6 (9, 12) sts, ch 1, turn, leaving rest of row unworked. Cont even until armhole measures approx 4$\frac{1}{2}$ (5, 5$\frac{1}{2}$)" from beg. Fasten off.

For second side of neck and buttonband, with RS facing and larger hook, skip the middle 33 (34, 35) sts, attach yarn with a slip st to next st and ch 1. Sc into same st as slip st, sc into 5 (8, 11) sc to end row. Cont even in sc on this side until armhole measures approx 5$\frac{1}{2}$ (6, 6$\frac{1}{2}$)". Fasten off.

FRONT BODICE
Work as for back until piece measures approx 4$\frac{1}{2}$ (5$\frac{1}{4}$, 6$\frac{1}{2}$)" from beg, ending after WS row. Ch 1, turn.

Shape Neck: Next Row (RS): Sc into first 16 (19, 22) sc, ch 1, turn, leaving rest of row unworked. Dec 1 st at neck edge every row eight times, then every other row twice—6 (9, 12) sts rem.

Cont even on these 6 (9, 12) sts until armhole measures approx 4 (4$\frac{1}{2}$, 5)". Place markers for one (two, three) evenly-spaced buttonholes along band, making the first and last $\frac{1}{4}$" from edges.

Next Row: Cont in sc, making one (two, three) buttonholes by working (ch 2, skip next 2 sc) where marked. Ch 1, turn.

Next Row: Cont in sc, working 2 sc into each ch-2 sp of the previous row. Ch 1, turn.

Cont even in sc until this side measures approx 7½ (8¼, 9½)" from beg. Fasten off.

For second side of neck, with RS facing and larger hook, skip the middle 13 (14, 15) sc, attach yarn with a slip st to next st and ch 1. Sc into same st as last slip st, sc into 15 (18, 21) sc to end row—16 (19, 22) sc. Ch 1, turn.

Cont in sc, and dec 1 st at neck edge every row eight times, then every other row twice—6 (9, 12) sc rem. Cont even until armhole on this side measures approx 7½ (8¼, 9½)". Fasten off.

SKIRT BACK

With RS facing and larger hook, attach B with a slip st to lower edge of back bodice and ch 1.

Row 1 (RS): Working into unused loops of foundation ch, sc into each ch across—65 (74, 83) sc. Ch 1, turn.

Row 2: Sc into each sc across. Ch 3, turn.

Row 3: Skip first sc, dc into next sc, *FPDC into next sc one row below, skip the sc behind the FPDC just made, skip next 2 sc, [(2-dc cluster, ch 3) twice, 2-dc cluster] into next sc, skip next 2 sc, FPDC into next sc one row below, skip the sc behind the FPDC just made, dc into next 2 sc. Repeat from * across. Ch 3, turn.

Row 4: Skip first dc, dc into next dc, *BPDC into next st, ch 3, skip next 2-dc cluster and ch-3 sp, sc into next 2-dc cluster, skip next ch-3 sp and 2-dc cluster, ch 3, BPDC into next st, dc into next 2 dc. Repeat from * across, ending row with BPDC into next st, ch 3, skip next 2-dc cluster and ch-3 sp, sc into next 2-dc cluster, skip next ch-3 sp and 2-dc cluster, ch 3, BPDC into next st, dc into next dc, dc into top of turning-ch-3. Ch 3, turn.

Row 5: Skip first dc, dc into next dc, *FPDC into next st, [(2-dc cluster, ch 3) twice, 2-dc cluster] into next sc, skip next ch-3 sp, FPDC into next st, dc into next 2 dc. Repeat from * across, ending row with FPDC into next st, [(2-dc cluster, ch 3) twice, 2-dc cluster] into next sc, skip next ch-3 sp, FPDC into next st, dc into next dc, dc into top of turning-ch-3. Ch 3, turn.

Rows 6-9: Same as Rows 4 and 5. Ch 3, turn.

Row 10 (Inc Row): Skip first dc, 2 dc into next dc, *BPDC into next st, ch 3, skip next 2-dc cluster and ch-3 sp, sc into next 2-dc cluster, skip next ch-3 sp and 2-dc cluster, ch 3, BPDC into next st, 2 dc into next 2 dc. Repeat from * across, ending row with BPDC into next st, ch 3, skip next 2-dc cluster and ch-3 sp, sc into next 2-dc cluster, skip next ch-3 sp and 2-dc cluster, ch 3, BPDC into next st, 2 dc into next dc, dc into top of turning-ch-3. Ch 3, turn.

Row 11: Skip first dc, dc into next 2 dc, *FPDC into next st, [(2-dc cluster, ch 3) twice, 2-dc cluster] into next sc, skip next ch-3 sp, FPDC into next st, dc into next 4 dc. Repeat from * across, ending row with FPDC into next st, [(2-dc cluster, ch 3) twice, 2-dc cluster] into next sc, skip next ch-3 sp, FPDC into next st, dc into next 2 dc, dc into top of turning-ch-3. Ch 3, turn.

Row 12: Skip first dc, dc into next 2 dc, *BPDC into next st, ch 3, skip next 2-dc cluster and ch-3 sp, sc into next 2-dc cluster, skip next ch-3 sp and 2-dc cluster, ch 3, BPDC into next st, dc into next 4 dc. Repeat from * across, ending row with BPDC into next st, ch 3, skip next 2-dc cluster and ch-3 sp, sc into next 2-dc cluster, skip next ch-3 sp and 2-dc cluster, ch 3, BPDC into next st, dc into next 2 dc, dc into top of turning-ch-3. Ch 3, turn.

Rows 13-16: As Rows 11 and 12. Ch 3, turn.

Row 17: As Row 11. Ch 3, turn.

Row 18 (Inc Row): Skip first dc, 2 dc into next dc, dc into next dc, *BPDC into next st, ch 3, skip next 2-dc cluster and ch-3 sp, sc into next 2-dc cluster, skip next ch-3 sp and 2-dc cluster, ch 3, BPDC into next st, 2 dc into next dc, dc into next 2 dc, 2 dc into next dc. Repeat from * across, ending row with BPDC into next st, ch 3, skip next 2-dc cluster and ch-3 sp, sc into next 2-dc cluster, skip next ch-3 sp and 2-dc cluster, ch 3, BPDC into next st, dc into next dc, 2 dc into next dc, dc into top of turning-ch-3. Ch 3, turn.

Row 19: Skip first dc, dc into next 3 dc, *FPDC into next st, [(2-dc cluster, ch 3) twice, 2-dc cluster] into next sc, skip next ch-3 sp, FPDC into next st, dc into next 6 dc. Repeat from * across, ending row with FPDC into next st, [(2-dc cluster, ch 3) twice, 2-dc cluster] into next sc, skip next ch-3 sp, FPDC into next st, dc into next 3 dc, dc into top of turning-ch-3. Ch 3, turn.

Row 20: Skip first dc, dc into next 3 dc, *BPDC into next st, ch 3, skip next 2-dc cluster and ch-3 sp, sc into next 2-dc cluster, skip next ch-3 sp and 2-dc cluster, ch 3, BPDC into next st, dc into next 6 dc. Repeat from * across, ending row with BPDC into next st, ch 3, skip next 2-dc cluster and ch-3 sp, sc into next 2-dc cluster, skip next ch-3 sp and 2-dc cluster, ch 3, BPDC into next st, dc into next 3 dc, dc into top of turning-ch-3. Ch 3, turn.

Rows 21-26: As Rows 19 and 20. Ch 3, turn.

Row 27: As Row 19. Ch 3, turn.

Row 28 (Inc Row): Skip first dc, 2 dc into next dc, dc into next 2 dc, *BPDC into next st, ch 3, skip next 2-dc cluster and ch-3 sp, sc into next 2-dc cluster, skip next ch-3 sp and 2-dc cluster, ch 3, BPDC into next st, 2 dc into next dc, dc into next 4 dc, 2 dc into next dc. Repeat from * across, ending row with BPDC into next st, ch 3, skip next 2-dc cluster and ch-3 sp, sc into next 2-dc cluster, skip next ch-3 sp and 2-dc cluster, ch 3, BPDC into next st, dc into next 2 dc, 2 dc into next dc, dc into top of turning-ch-3. Ch 3, turn.

Row 29: Skip first dc, dc into next 4 dc, *FPDC into next st, [(2-dc cluster, ch 3) twice, 2-dc cluster] into next sc, skip next ch-3 sp, FPDC into next st, dc into next 8 dc. Repeat from * across, ending row with FPDC into next st, [(2-dc cluster, ch 3) twice, 2-dc cluster] into next sc, skip next ch-3 sp, FPDC into next st, dc into next 4 dc, dc into top of turning-ch-3. Ch 3, turn.

Row 30: Skip first dc, dc into next 4 dc *BPDC into next st, ch 3, skip next 2-dc cluster and ch-3 sp, sc into next 2-dc cluster, skip next ch-3 sp and 2-dc cluster, ch 3, BPDC into next st, dc into next 8 dc. Repeat from * across, ending row with BPDC into next st, ch 3, skip next 2-dc cluster and ch-3 sp, sc into next 2-dc cluster, skip next ch-3 sp and 2-dc cluster, ch 3, BPDC into next st, dc into next 4 dc, dc into top of turning-ch-3. Ch 3, turn.

Repeat Rows 29 and 30 until piece measures approx 11" from beg, ending after WS row. Ch 1, turn.

Next Row (RS): Sc into first 5 dc, *sc into next FPDC, [(2-dc cluster, ch 3) twice, 2-dc cluster] into next sc, sc into next FPDC, sc into next 8 sc. Repeat from * across, ending row with sc into next FPDC, [(2-dc cluster, ch 3) twice, 2-dc cluster] into next sc, sc into next FPDC, sc into last 4 dc, sc into top of turning-ch-3. Fasten off.

SKIRT FRONT

With RS facing and larger hook, attach B with a slip st to lower edge of front bodice and ch 1. Complete as for back skirt.

FINISHING

Sew right shoulder seam.

Neckband: With RS facing and smaller hook, attach B with a slip st to neck edge of buttonhole band and ch 1.

Row 1 (RS): Work 96 (99, 102) sc evenly around neckline, including sides of buttonband and buttonhole band. Ch 1, turn.

Row 2: Sc into each sc. Ch 1, turn.

Row 3: Sc into first 3 sc, *ch 3, slip st into top of fourth st from hook, sc into next 3 sc. Repeat from * around. Fasten off.

Sew side seams.

Left Armhole Band: With RS facing and smaller hook, attach B with a slip st to armhole edge of buttonband.

Row 1 (RS): Work 75 (78, 81) sc evenly around armhole, including sides of buttonband and buttonhole band. Ch 1, turn.

Rows 2 and 3: Same as Rows 2 and 3 of neckband. Fasten off.

Right Armhole Band: With RS facing and smaller hook, attach B with a slip st to top of side seam and ch 1.

Rnd 1 (RS): Work 69 (72, 75) sc evenly around armhole. Join with a slip st to first sc. Ch 1, turn.

Rnd 2: Sc into each sc. Join with a slip st to first sc. Ch 1, turn.

Rnd 3: Sc into first 3 sc, *ch 3, slip st into top of fourth st from hook, sc into next 3 sc. Repeat from * around, ending rnd with slip st to first sc. Fasten off.

Leaves: With smaller hook and C, ch 8. Sc into second ch from hook, hdc into next ch, dc into next ch, tr into next ch, dc into next ch, hdc into next ch, sc into next ch, ch 7, turn; working into the ch-7 just made, sc into second ch from hook, hdc into next ch, dc into next ch, tr into next ch, dc into next ch, hdc into next ch, slip st into the unused loop of foundation ch below the first sc made. Fasten off, leaving a 6" tail.

Rose: With smaller hook and B, ch 9. 2 dc into fourth ch from hook, *3 dc into next ch. Repeat from * across until 1 ch remains, ending row with (2 dc, ch 3, slip st) into last ch. Fasten off, leaving a 6" tail.

Sew leaves onto RS of front, 1" down from center front of neck. Sew rose onto the center of leaves. Sew on buttons.

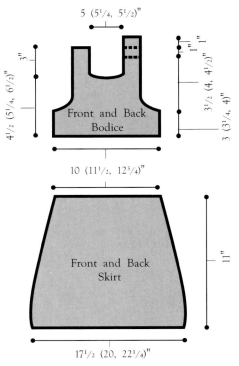

Baby's Dainty Cardigan

INTERMEDIATE SKILL LEVEL

SIZES

Infant's size 6 (12, 18) months. Instructions are for smallest size, with changes for other sizes noted in parentheses as necessary.

FINISHED MEASUREMENTS

Chest (Buttoned): 22$^{1}/_{2}$ (23$^{1}/_{4}$, 27$^{1}/_{4}$)"
Length (Before edging): 11 (12$^{1}/_{2}$, 13$^{1}/_{2}$)"
Sleeve width at underarm: 10 (10$^{3}/_{4}$, 10$^{3}/_{4}$)"

MATERIALS

Coats and Clark's *Red Heart Baby Fingering Pompadour* (fingering weight, 84% acrylic/16% olefin; 1$^{4}/_{5}$ oz; approx 270 yds), 4 (4, 5) skeins Baby Yellow #224
Crochet hook, sizes C/2 and D/3 or size needed to obtain gauge
One $^{3}/_{4}$" button (JHB International's *Saipan Style #17172* was used on sample garment)

GAUGE

With larger hook in Lace Patt, each (2 dc, ch 2, 2 dc) shell measures $^{3}/_{4}$" across, and 12 rows = 4".
To measure your gauge, make a test swatch as follows: With larger hook, ch 32.
Work Lace Patt on 5 shells for twelve rows total. Fasten off.
Piece should measure 4$^{1}/_{2}$" wide and 4" long. **To save time, take time to check gauge.**

NOTES

Dec sc = (Insert hook into next st and pull up a loop) twice, yarn over and draw it through all three loops on hook.
Shell = (2 dc, ch 2, 2 dc).

LACE PATT

(Ch mult. 6 + 2)
Foundation Row (RS): Sc into second ch from hook, *skip next 2 ch, (2 dc, ch 2, 2 dc) into next ch, skip next 2 ch, sc into next ch. Repeat from * across. Ch 5, turn.
Row 1 (WS): *Sc into next ch-2 sp, ch 2, dc into next sc, ch 2. Repeat from * across, ending row with sc into next ch-2 sp, dc into last sc. Ch 1, turn.
Row 2: Sc into first dc, *(2 dc, ch 2, 2 dc) into next sc, sc into next dc. Repeat from * across, ending row with (2 dc, ch 2, 2 dc) into next sc, sc into third ch of turning-ch-5. Ch 5, turn. Repeat Rows 1 and 2 for patt.

BACK

With larger hook, ch 74 (86, 92). Beg Lace Patt, and work even on 12 (14, 15) shells until piece measures approx 11 (12$^{1}/_{2}$, 13$^{1}/_{2}$)" from beg, ending after WS row. Fasten off.

LEFT FRONT

With larger hook, ch 38 (44, 44). Beg Lace Patt, and work even on 6 (7, 7) shells until piece measures approx 8$^{1}/_{2}$ (10, 11)" from beg, ending after WS row. Ch 1, turn.

Shape Neck: Neck Dec Row 1 (RS): Sc into first dc, *(2 dc, ch 2, 2 dc) into next sc, sc into next dc. Repeat from * three (four, four) *more* times, ending row with 2 dc into next sc. Ch 3, turn, leaving rest of row unworked.

Neck Dec Row 2: *Dc into next sc, ch 2, sc into next ch-2 sp, ch 2. Repeat from * across, ending row with dc into last sc. Ch 1, turn.

Neck Dec Row 3: Sc into first dc, *(2 dc, ch 2, 2 dc) into next sc, sc into next dc. Repeat from * three (four, four) *more* times. Ch 4, turn, leaving rest of row unworked.

Neck Dec Row 4: *Sc into next ch-2 sp, ch 2, dc into next sc, ch 2. Repeat from * across, ending row with sc into next ch-2 sp, ch 2, dc into last sc. Ch 1, turn.

Neck Dec Row 5: Sc into first dc, *(2 dc, ch 2, 2 dc) into next sc, sc into next dc. Repeat from * two (three, three) *more* times, ending row with 2 dc into next sc. Ch 3, turn, leaving rest of row unworked.

Neck Dec Row 6: Same as Neck Dec Row 2.

Neck Dec Row 7: Sc into first dc, *(2 dc, ch 2, 2 dc) into next sc, sc into next dc. Repeat from * two (three, three) *more* times. Ch 4, turn, leaving rest of row unworked.

Neck Dec Row 8: Same as Neck Dec Row 4—3 (4, 4) shells rem. Fasten off.

RIGHT FRONT

Work as for left front until piece measures approx 8½ (10, 11)" from beg, ending after WS row. *Do not ch 1 to turn.*

Shape Neck: Neck Dec Row 1 (RS): Slip st into first 10 sts, ch 3, dc into same st as slip st, sc into next dc, *(2 dc, ch 2, 2 dc) into next sc, sc into next dc. Repeat from * three (four, four) *more* times. Ch 5, turn.

Neck Dec Row 2: *Sc into next ch-2 sp, ch 2, dc into next sc, ch 2. Repeat from * three (four, four) *more* times, ending row with sc into top of turning-ch-3. Turn.

Neck Dec Row 3: Slip st into first 4 sts, ch 1, sc into same st as slip st, *(2 dc, ch 2, 2 dc) into next sc, sc into next dc. Repeat from * three (four, four) *more* times. Ch 5, turn.

Neck Dec Row 4: *Sc into next ch-2 sp, ch 2, dc into next sc, ch 2. Repeat from * two (three, three) *more* times, ending row with sc into next ch-2 sp, ch 1, dc into last sc. Turn.

Neck Dec Row 5: Slip st into first 3 sts, ch 3, dc into same st as slip st, sc into next dc, *(2 dc, ch 2, 2 dc) into next sc, sc into next dc. Repeat from * two (three, three) *more* times. Ch 5, turn.

Neck Dec Row 6: *Sc into next ch-2 sp, ch 2, dc into next sc, ch 2. Repeat from * two (three, three) *more* times, ending row with sc into top of turning-ch-3. Turn.

Neck Dec Row 7: Slip st into first 4 sts, ch 1, sc into same st as slip st, *(2 dc, ch 2, 2 dc) into next sc, sc into next dc. Repeat from * two (three, three) *more* times. Ch 5, turn.

Neck Dec Row 8: *Sc into next ch-2 sp, ch 2, dc into next sc, ch 2. Repeat from * one (two, two) *more* times, ending row with sc into next ch-2 sp, ch 1, dc into last sc. Fasten off.

SLEEVES

With larger hook, ch 44 (50, 50). Work one (one, three) rows of Lace Patt on 7 (8, 8) shells. Ch 3, turn.

Sleeve Inc Row 1 (WS): Dc into first sc, *ch 2, sc into next ch-2 sp, ch 2, dc into next sc. Repeat from * across, ending row with ch 2, sc into next ch-2 sp, ch 2, 2 dc into last sc. Ch 3, turn.

Sleeve Inc Row 2: 2 Hdc into first dc, *sc into next dc, (2 dc, ch 2, 2 dc) into next sc. Repeat from * across, ending row with sc into next dc, (2 hdc, dc) into top of turning-ch-3. Ch 1, turn.

Sleeve Inc Row 3: Sc into first dc, skip next 2 hdc, *ch 2, dc into next sc, ch 2, sc into next ch-2 sp. Repeat from * across, ending row with ch 2, dc into next sc, ch 2, dc into next sc, ch 2, sc into top of turning-ch-3. Ch 3, turn.

Sleeve Inc Row 4: (Dc, ch 2, 2 dc) into first sc, *sc into next dc, *(2 dc, ch 2, 2 dc) into next sc. Repeat from * across. Ch 5, turn.

Sleeve Inc Row 5: *Sc into next ch-2 sp, ch 2, dc into next sc, ch 2. Repeat from * across, ending row with sc into next ch-2 sp, ch 2, dc into top of turning-ch-3. Ch 1, turn.

Sleeve Inc Row 6: Sc into first dc, *(2 dc, ch 2, 2 dc) into next sc, sc into next dc. Repeat from * across, ending row with (2 dc, ch 2, 2 dc) into next sc, sc into third ch of turning-ch-5. Ch 5, turn.

Next two (four, six) Rows: Work even in Lace Patt on 9 (10, 10) shells. After last row, ch 3, turn.

Repeat Sleeve Inc Rows 1-6 once *more*. Work even in Lace Patt on 11 (12, 12) shells until piece measures approx 6¼ (7¼, 8½)" from beg, ending after WS row. Fasten off.

FINISHING

Back Lower Border: With RS facing and smaller hook, attach yarn with a slip st to first sc and ch 1.

Row 1 (RS): Working along opposite side of foundation ch, sc into each ch across—73 (85, 91) sc. Ch 1, turn.

Next Row: Sc into each sc across. Ch 1, turn.

Next Row: Sc into first sc, *ch 3, 2 dc into same place as last sc, skip next 2 sc, sc into next sc. Repeat from * across. Fasten off.

Front Lower Borders: With RS facing and smaller hook, attach yarn with a slip st to first sc and ch 1. Complete as for back lower border—37 (43, 43) sts.

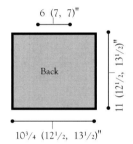

6 (7, 7)"

Back

11 (12½, 13½)"

10¾ (12½, 13½)"

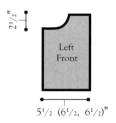

2½"

Left Front

5½ (6½, 6½)"

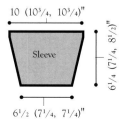

10 (10¾, 10¾)"

Sleeve

6¼ (7¼, 8½)"

6½ (7¼, 7¼)"

Sew shoulder seams. Set in sleeves. Sew sleeve and side seams.

Sleeve Lower Borders: With RS facing and smaller hook, attach yarn with a slip st to lower sleeve seam and ch 1.

Rnd 1 (RS): Working along opposite side of foundation ch, sc into each ch around—43 (49, 49) sts. Join with slip st to first sc. Ch 1, turn.

Rnd 2: Sc into each sc around. Join with slip st to first sc. Ch 1, turn.

Rnd 3: Sc into first sc, *ch 3, 2 dc into same place as last sc, skip next 2 sc, sc into next sc. Repeat from * around. Join with slip st to first sc. Fasten off.

Front Edges: With RS facing, attach yarn to lower right front edge and ch 1.

Row 1 (RS): Work sc evenly along right front edge, around neckline, and down left front edge, working dec sc at both shoulders. Ch 1, turn.

Row 2: Same as last row, working (ch 5, skip 3 sc) at right front neck edge for buttonloop. Fasten off.

Sew on button.

striped duo

$\mathcal{F}$un and fresh, these two sporty sweaters are as easy to make as they are to wear!

Child's Crewneck Pullover

INTERMEDIATE SKILL LEVEL

SIZES
Child's size 8 (10, 12, 14). Instructions are for smallest size, with changes for other sizes noted in parentheses as necessary.

FINISHED MEASUREMENTS
Chest: 34 (36, 38, 40)"
Length: 16 (17, 18, 19)"
Sleeve width at underarm: 14 (15, 16, 17)"

MATERIALS
Caron International's *Simply Soft* (worsted weight, 100% acrylic; 6 oz; approx 330 yds), 2 (2, 3, 4) skeins Red Violet #9718 (A), 2 (3, 3, 4) skeins Off-White #9702 (B), and 1 (1, 2, 2) skeins Royale #9713 (C)
Crochet hooks, sizes G/6 and H/8 or size needed to obtain gauge

GAUGE
In V-St Patt, with larger hook, 20 sts and 12 rows = 5".
To measure your gauge, make a test swatch as follows: With larger hook, ch 23.
Work even in V-St Patt for twelve rows. Fasten off.
Piece should measure 5" square. **To save time, take time to check gauge.**

NOTES
V-St = 2 dc into same space.
Each turning-ch-3 counts as a dc throughout.
Dec sc = (Insert hook into next st and pull up a loop) twice, yarn over and draw it through all three loops on hook.

Dec dc = (Yarn over, insert hook into next st and pull up a loop, yarn over and draw it through two loops on hook) twice, yarn over and draw it through all three loops on hook.
To change color, work until 2 loops rem on hook; with the new color, complete the st; fasten off the old color.

V-ST PATT
(Ch mult. 2 + 1)
Foundation Row (RS): 2 Dc into fifth ch from hook, *skip next ch, 2 dc into next ch. Repeat from * across, ending row with skip next ch, dc into last ch. Ch 3, turn.
Patt Row: Skip first dc, *2 dc into space between next 2 dc, skip next 2 dc. Repeat from * across, ending row with dc into top of turning-ch-3. Ch 3, turn.
Repeat Patt Row.

STRIPE PATT
*3 Rows A, 1 row B, 1 row C, 1 row B. Repeat from * for patt.

BACK
With larger hook and A, ch 71 (75, 79, 83). Beg V-St Patt—33 (35, 37, 39) V-Sts plus one dc each side.

Work even in Stripe Patt until piece measures approx 15 (16, 17, 18)" from beg, ending after WS row. Ch 3, turn.

Shape Neck: Next Row (RS): V-St into next 11 (12, 12, 13) V-Sts, dc into space between next 2 sts, ch 3, turn, leaving rest of row unworked. Cont even in patt as established on this side until piece measures 16 (17, 18, 19)" from beg. Fasten off.

For second side of neck, with RS facing, skip the middle nine (nine, eleven, eleven) V-Sts, attach yarn with a slip st into space between next 2 sts and ch 3. Cont in patt as established to end row. Complete as for first side.

FRONT
Work as for back until piece measures approx 14 (15, 16, 17)" from beg, ending after WS row. Ch 3, turn.

Shape Neck: Next Row (RS): V-St into next 11 (12, 12, 13) V-Sts, dc into space in middle of next V-St, yarn over, insert hook into same place as last dc and pull up a loop, yarn over and draw it through two loops on hook, skip next 2 dc, yarn over, insert hook into space before next dc and pull up a loop, yarn over and draw it through two loops on hook, yarn over and draw it through all three loops on hook (dec-st just made). Ch 3, turn, leaving rest of row unworked.

Next Row: Skip dec st and next 2 dc, dc into space before next dc, *skip next 2 dc, V-St before next dc. Repeat from * across, ending row with dc into top of turning-ch-3. Ch 3, turn.

Next Row: V-St into next 10 (11, 11, 12) V-Sts, skip next dc, dc into next dc. Ch 3, turn, leaving turning-ch-3 unworked.

Cont even until this side measures same as back. Fasten off.

For second side of neck, with RS facing, skip the middle seven (seven, nine, nine) V-Sts, attach yarn with a slip st into space between next 2 sts and ch 3.

Next Row (RS): Skip 2 dc, dc into space before next dc, yarn over, insert hook into same space as last dc and pull up a loop, yarn over and draw it through two loops on hook, skip next 2 dc, yarn over, insert hook into space before next dc and pull up a loop, yarn over and draw it through 2 loops on hook, yarn over and draw it through 3 loops on hook (dec-st made), dc into same space as dec-st, cont in patt as established to end row. Ch 3, turn.

Next Row: V-St into next 10 (11, 11, 12) V-Sts, skip next 2 dc, dec dc to combine the space before the next dc and the top of turning-ch-3. Ch 3, turn.

Next Row: Skip first dec dc, and cont in patt as established to end row. Ch 3, turn.

Complete as for first side.

SLEEVES

With larger hook and A, ch 31 (31, 35, 35). Work two rows of V-St Patt—13 (13, 15, 15) V-Sts plus one dc each side. Ch 3, turn.

Inc Row 1 (RS): Dc into first dc, skip next dc, *2 dc into space before next dc, skip next 2 dc. Repeat from * across, ending row with 2 dc into space before next dc, skip next dc, 2 dc into top of turning-ch-3. Change color, ch 3, turn.

Inc Row 2: Skip first dc, dc into space before next dc, *skip next 2 dc, 2 dc into space before next dc. Repeat from * across, ending row with skip next 2 dc, 2 dc under turning-ch-3. Change color, ch 3, turn.

Inc Row 3: Skip first dc, *2 dc into space before next dc, skip next 2 dc. Repeat from * across, ending row with 2 dc under turning-ch-3, dc into top of turning-ch-3. Change color, ch 3, turn.

Inc Row 4: Skip first 2 dc, *2 dc into space before next dc, skip next 2 dc. Repeat from * across, ending row with 2 dc into space before next dc, dc into top of turning-ch-3. Change color, ch 3, turn.

Cont in Stripe Patt, and repeat Inc Rows 1-4 six (seven, seven, eight) *more* times—27 (29, 31, 33) V-Sts plus one dc each side.

Cont even until piece measures approx 13½ (15, 16, 17½)" from beg. Fasten off.

FINISHING

Sew shoulder seams.

Neckband: With RS facing and smaller hook, work two rnds of sc around neckline, working dec sc at beg of neck shaping on both sides of front and back. Fasten off.

Place markers 7 (7½, 8, 8½)" down from shoulders. Set in sleeves between markers. Sew sleeve and side seams.

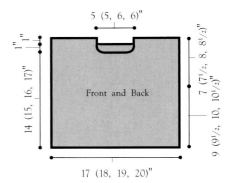

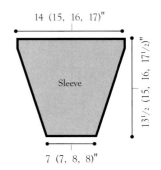

Child's Rugby Pullover

INTERMEDIATE SKILL LEVEL

SIZES

Child's size 8 (10, 12, 14). Instructions are for smallest size, with changes for other sizes noted in parentheses as necessary.

FINISHED MEASUREMENTS

Chest: 34 (37, 39, 40$\frac{1}{2}$)"
Length: 20 (21, 22, 23)"
Sleeve width at underarm: 16 (18, 19, 20)"

MATERIALS

Caron International's *Simply Soft* (worsted weight, 100% acrylic; 6 oz; approx 330 yds), 4 (5, 5, 6) skeins Royale #9713 (A), 1 skein *each* Off-White #9702 (B) and Country Blue #9710 (C)
Crochet hooks, sizes G/6 and H/8 or size needed to obtain gauge
One 7" zipper (Coats' *Sport Zipper Art. #F. 45* was used on sample garment)

GAUGE

With larger hook, in Seed St Patt, 25 sts = 5" and 17 rows = 4".
To measure your gauge, make a test swatch as follows: With larger hook, ch 26.
Work Seed St Patt for seventeen rows. Fasten off.
Piece should measure 5" wide and 4" long. **To save time, take time to check gauge.**

NOTES

Each sc and ch-1 sp counts as one st.
Dec sc = (Insert hook into next st and pull up a loop) twice, yarn over and draw it through all three loops on hook.

RIB PATT

(Over an odd number of ch)
Foundation Row (RS): Dc into fourth ch from hook and into each ch across. Ch 2, turn.
Row 1 (WS): Skip first st, *FPDC into next st, BPDC into next st. Repeat from * across, ending row with FPDC into next st, hdc into top of turning-ch. Ch 2, turn.
Row 2: Skip first st, *BPDC into next st, FPDC into next st. Repeat from * across, ending row with BPDC into next st, hdc into top of turning-ch-2. Ch 2, turn.
Repeat Rows 1 and 2 for patt.

SEED ST PATT

(Mult. 2 + 1 sts)
Foundation Row (RS): Sc into first st, *ch 1, skip next st, sc into next st. Repeat from * across. Ch 1, turn.
Row 1 (WS): Sc into first sc and ch-1 sp, *ch 1, skip next sc, sc into next ch-1 sp. Repeat from * across, ending row with sc into last sc. Ch 1, turn.
Row 2: Sc into first sc, *ch 1, skip next sc, sc into next ch-1 sp. Repeat from * across, ending row with ch 1, skip next sc, sc into last sc. Ch 1, turn.
Repeat Rows 1 and 2 for patt.

BACK

With smaller hook and A, ch 87 (95, 99, 103). Work Rib Patt until piece measures approx 2" from beg, ending after WS row—85 (93, 97, 101) sts each row. Change to larger hook, ch 1, turn.

Next Row (RS): Work Foundation Row of Seed St Patt—85 (93, 97, 101) sts. Ch 1, turn.

Cont even in Seed St Patt with A until piece measures approx 10$\frac{1}{2}$ (10$\frac{1}{2}$, 11, 11$\frac{1}{2}$)" from beg, ending after WS row.

Beg Stripe: Next Row (RS): Cont in Seed St Patt as established, work one row B, seven rows C, one row B, five rows A, one row B, seven rows C, one row B.

Cont even with A until piece measures approx 20 (21, 22, 23)" from beg. Fasten off.

FRONT

Work same as back until piece measures approx 13 (14, 15, 16)" from beg, ending after WS row.

Divide for Zipper Opening: Next Row (RS): Work patt as established across first 41 (45, 47, 49) sts, ch 1, turn, leaving rest of row unworked.

Cont even on this side until piece measures approx 17$\frac{1}{2}$ (18$\frac{1}{2}$, 19$\frac{1}{2}$, 20$\frac{1}{2}$)" from beg, ending after WS row.

Shape Neck: Next Row (RS): Work across first 31 (35, 37, 39) sts, work a dec sc to combine the next sc and ch-1 sp, leaving rest of row unworked—32 (36, 38, 40) sts.

Neck Dec Row 1 (WS): Dec sc to combine the first dec sc and sc, cont in patt as established to end row. Ch 1, turn.

Neck Dec Row 2: Work patt as established until 2 sts rem, ending row with dec sc to combine the last 2 sts. Ch 1, turn.

Repeat last two rows twice *more*, then work Neck Dec Row 1 once *more*—25 (29, 31, 33) sts rem.

Cont even until this side measures approx 20 (21, 22, 23)" from beg. Fasten off.

For second side of neck, with RS facing, skip the middle 3 sts, attach A with a slip st to next st and ch 1. Work patt as established across next 41 (45, 47, 49) sts. Ch 3, turn.

Cont even on this side until piece measures approx 17$\frac{1}{2}$ (18$\frac{1}{2}$, 19$\frac{1}{2}$, 20$\frac{1}{2}$)" from beg, ending after WS row. *Do not ch 1 to turn.*

Shape Neck: Next Row (RS): Slip st into first 9 sts, ch 1, dec sc to combine the next ch-1 sp and sc, cont patt as established to end row—31 (35, 37, 39) sts. Ch 1, turn.

Neck Dec Row 1 (WS): Work patt as established until 2 sts rem in row, ending row with dec sc to combine the last sc and sc dec. Ch 1, turn.

Neck Dec Row 2: Dec sc to combine the first dec sc and sc, cont in patt as established to end row. Ch 1, turn.

Repeat last two rows twice *more*, then work Neck Dec Row 1 once *more*—25 (29, 31, 33) sts rem. Complete same as first side.

SLEEVES

With smaller hook and A, ch 37 (37, 43, 47). Work Rib Patt until piece measures approx 2" from beg, ending after WS row—35 (35, 41, 45) sts each row. Change to larger hook, ch 1, turn.

For size 10 only:
Next Row: 2 Sc into first st, *ch 1, skip next st, sc into next st. Repeat from * across, ending row with ch 1, skip next st, 2 sc into last st. Ch 1, turn.

Repeat last row three *more* times—43 sts.

For all sizes:
Inc Row 1: Sc into first st, *ch 1, skip next st, sc into next st. Repeat from * across, ending row with sc into last st. Ch 1, turn.

Inc Row 2: 2 Sc into first sc, sc into next ch-1 sp, *ch 1, skip next sc, sc into next ch-1 sp. Repeat from * across, ending row with 2 sc into last sc. Ch 1, turn.

Inc Row 3: Sc into first 2 sc, *ch 1, skip next sc, sc into next ch-1 sp. Repeat from * across, ending row with ch 1, skip next sc, sc into last 2 sc. Ch 1, turn.

Inc Row 4: 2 Sc into first sc, *ch 1, skip next sc, sc into next ch-1 sp. Repeat from * across, ending row with ch 1, skip next sc, 2 sc into last sc. Ch 1, turn.

Repeat last four rows 10 (11, 12, 11) *more* times—79 (91, 93, 93) sts.

For size 8 and 12 only:
Repeat Inc Rows 1 and 2 once *more*—81(95) sts.

For size 14 only:
Next Row: Sc into first st, *ch 1, skip next st, sc into next st. Repeat from * across, ending row with sc into last st. Ch 1, turn.

Next Row: 2 Sc into first sc, sc into next ch-1 sp, *ch 1, skip next sc, sc into next ch-1 sp. Repeat from * across, ending row with 2 sc into last sc. Ch 1, turn.

Next Row: Sc into first 2 sc, *ch 1, skip next sc, sc into next ch-1 sp. Repeat from * across, ending row with ch 1, skip next sc, sc into last 2 sc. Ch 1, turn.

Next Row: Sc into first sc, *ch 1, skip next sc, sc into next ch-1 sp. Repeat from * across, ending row with ch 1, skip next sc, sc into last sc. Ch 1, turn.

Next Row: Sc into first sc and ch-1 sp, *ch 1, skip next sc, sc into next ch-1 sp. Repeat from * across, ending row with sc into last sc.

Next Row: 2 Sc into first sc, *ch 1, skip next sc, sc into next ch-1 sp. Repeat from * across, ending row with ch 1, skip next sc, 2 sc into last sc. Ch 1, turn.

Next Row: Sc into first sc, *ch 1, skip next st, sc into next st. Repeat from * across, ending row with sc into last st. Ch 1, turn.

Next Row: Sc into first sc and ch-1 sp, *ch 1, skip next sc, sc into next ch-1 sp. Repeat from * across, ending row with sc into last sc.

Repeat last 8 rows one *more* time—101 sts.

For all sizes:
Cont even in patt on 81 (91, 95, 101) sts until piece measures approx 14 (15¹⁄₄, 16¹⁄₄, 18)" from beg. Fasten off.

FINISHING
Sew shoulder seams.

Neckband: With RS facing, and smaller hook, attach A with a slip st to beg of neck shaping on right front and ch 3. Work 66 dc along neck edge—67 sts including ch-3. Ch 2, turn.

Repeat Rows 1 and 2 of Rib Patt until neckband measures approx 2¹⁄₂" from beg. Fasten off.

Zipper Facing: With RS facing and smaller hook, attach A with a slip st to top LH side of zipper opening and ch 1. Work one row of sc around zipper opening, working a dec sc at each lower corner of opening. Fasten off.

Sew in zipper.

Place markers 8 (9, 9¹⁄₂, 10)" down from shoulders. Set in sleeves between markers. Sew sleeve and side seams.

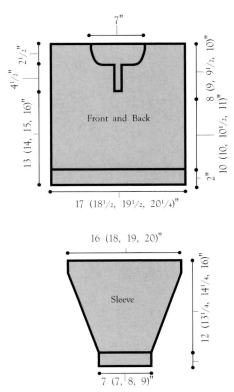

harvest time

In these three designs, autumnal colors warm both body and soul. Plus, their textured stitch patterns are great fun to work.

Man's Two-Toned Pullover

INTERMEDIATE SKILL LEVEL

SIZES
Man's Small (Medium, Large, Extra-Large). Instructions are for smallest size, with changes for other sizes noted in parentheses as necessary.

FINISHED MEASUREMENTS
Chest: 44 (48½, 53, 57)"
Length: 26¾ (27¼, 28, 28½)"
Sleeve width at underarm: 19 (20, 21, 22)"

MATERIALS
Caron's *Simply Soft* (worsted weight, 100% acrylic; 6 oz; approx 330 yds), 5 (5, 6, 6) skeins Java #9734 (A) and 4 (4, 5, 5) skeins Cedar #9704 (B)
Crochet hooks, sizes G/6 and H/8 or size needed to obtain gauge

GAUGE
With larger hook, in Spiked Patt, 15 sts and 19 rows = 4".
To measure your gauge, make a test swatch as follows: With larger hook and A, ch 16. Sc into second ch from hook and into each ch across. Ch 1, turn.
Beg with Foundation Row 2, work Spiked Patt for 18 rows. Fasten off. Piece should measure 4" square. **To save time, take time to check gauge.**

NOTES
To decrease, work a dec sc to combine the first 2 sts and the last 2 sts of the row.

Dec sc = (Insert hook into next st and pull up a loop) twice, yarn over and draw it through all three loops on hook.
To increase, work 2 sts into one st.
To change color, work until 2 loops rem on hook; with the new color, complete the st; fasten off the old color.
Long dc = Elongated dc worked into next st three rows below. On Foundation Row 3, work each long dc into the next ch of the Foundation Row 1 two rows below. Always skip one stitch underneath each long dc from the previous row.
Triple dec FPDC = *Yarn over and insert hook as for BPDC, yarn over and pull up a loop, yarn over and draw it through two loops on hook**; yarn over and insert hook as for FPDC into next st, yarn over and pull up a loop, yarn over and draw it through two loops on hook; repeat from * to ** once *more*, yarn over and draw it through all four remaining loops on hook.

RIB PATT
(*Over an even number of ch*)
Foundation Row (RS): Dc into fourth ch from hook and into each ch across. Ch 2, turn.
Row 1 (WS): Skip first st, *FPDC into next st, BPDC into next st. Repeat from * across, ending row with hdc into top of turning-ch. Ch 2, turn.
Row 2: Skip first st, *FPDC into next st, BPDC into next st. Repeat from * across, ending row with hdc into top of turning-ch-2. Ch 2, turn.
Repeat Rows 1 and 2 for patt.

SPIKED PATT
(*Mult. 4 + 3 sts*)
Foundation Row 1 (RS): With A, sc into each st across. Ch 1, turn.
Foundation Row 2: As last row. Change to B, ch 1, turn.
Foundation Row 3: With B, sc into first 3 sc, *long dc into foundation ch at base of next sc two rows below, sc into next 3 sc. Repeat from * across. Ch 1, turn.
Foundation Row 4: Sc into each st across. Change to A, ch 1, turn.
Row 1 (WS): With A, sc into first sc, *long dc, sc into next 3 sc. Repeat from * across, ending row with long dc, sc into last sc. Ch 1, turn.
Row 2: Sc into each st across. Change to B, ch 1, turn.
Row 3: With B, sc into first 3 sc, *long dc, sc into next 3 sc. Repeat from * across. Ch 1, turn.
Row 4: Same as Row 2. Change to A, ch 1, turn.
Repeat Rows 1-4 for patt.

BACK
With smaller hook and A, ch 84 (92, 100, 108). Work Rib Patt until piece measures approx 2½" from beg, ending after WS row—82 (90, 98, 106) sts each row. Change to larger hook, ch 1, turn.

Next Row: Beg Spiked Patt, inc 1 st at beg of Foundation Row 1—83 (91, 99, 107) sts.

Cont even until piece measures approx 17¼ (17¼, 17½, 17½)" from beg, ending after two rows worked with B (B, A, A). Ch 1, turn.

Shape Armholes: Cont in Spiked Patt as established, dec 1 st each side every row four times—75 (83, 91, 99) sts rem.

Work even until piece measures approx 25³⁄₄ (26¹⁄₄, 27, 27¹⁄₂)" from beg, ending after RS row. Ch 1, turn.

Shape Neck: Next Row (WS): Cont in Spiked Patt as established, work across first 24 (28, 30, 34) sts, ch 1, turn, leaving rest of row unworked. Cont even on this side until piece measures 26³⁄₄ (27¹⁄₄, 28, 28¹⁄₂)" from beg. Fasten off.

For second side of neck, with WS facing, skip the middle 27 (27, 31, 31) sts, attach yarn with a slip st to next st and ch 1. Complete as for first side.

FRONT

Work as for back until piece measures approx 19³⁄₄ (20¹⁄₄, 21, 21¹⁄₂)" from beg, ending after WS row. Ch 1, turn.

Shape Neck: Next Row (RS): Cont in Spiked Patt as established, and work across first 37 (41, 45, 49) sts, ch 1, turn, leaving rest of row unworked. Dec 1 st at neck edge every row 0 (0, 4, 4) times, then every other row 13 (13, 11, 11) times—24 (28, 30, 34) sts rem. Cont even on this side until it measures same as back to shoulders. Fasten off.

For second side of neck, with RS facing, skip the middle st and attach yarn with a slip st to next dc and ch 1. Complete as for first side.

SLEEVES

With smaller hook and A, ch 48 (48, 52, 52). Work Rib Patt until piece measures approx 2¹⁄₂" from beg, ending after WS row—46 (46, 50, 50) sts each row. Change to larger hook, ch 1, turn.

Next Row: Beg Spiked Patt, inc 1 st at beg of Foundation Row 1—47 (47, 51, 51) sts.

Cont in Spiked Patt as established, and inc 1 st each side every fourth row 0 (4, 5, 11) times, then every sixth row 10 (10, 9, 5) times, then every eighth row 2 (0, 0, 0) times—71 (75, 79, 83) sts. Cont even until sleeve measures approx 19¹⁄₂ (19¹⁄₂, 19¹⁄₄, 19¹⁄₄)" from beg, ending after two rows worked with B (B, A, A).

Shape Cap: Dec 1 st each side every row five times—61 (65, 69, 73) sts rem. Fasten off.

FINISHING

Sew shoulder seams.

Neckband: With RS facing and smaller hook, attach A with a slip st to neck edge of left shoulder seam and ch 3.

Rnd 1: Work 33 (33, 35, 35) dc along left front neck edge, work one dc at center front of neck, work 34 (34, 36, 36) dc along right front neck edge, then work 27 (27, 31, 31) dc along back of neck. Join with a slip st to top of ch-3. Ch 2. *Do not turn.* Place marker on center front st.

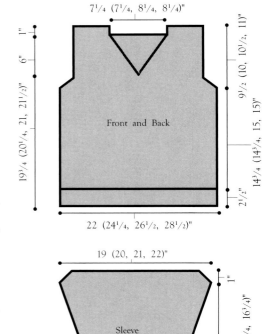

Rnd 2: Skip first st, *FPDC into next st, BPDC into next st. Repeat from * around, ending rnd with FPDC into next st, slip st to top of ch-2. Ch 2.

Rnd 3: Skip first st, *FPDC into next st, BPDC into next st. Repeat from * until one st before marked center front st; work a triple dec FPDC to combine the next 3 sts; complete same as last rnd. Join with a slip st to top of ch-3. Fasten off.

Set in sleeves. Sew sleeve and side seams.

Woman's Mélange Pullover

INTERMEDIATE SKILL LEVEL

SIZES

Woman's Small (Medium, Large, Extra-Large). Instructions are for smallest size, with changes for other sizes noted in parentheses as necessary.

FINISHED MEASUREMENTS

Bust: 39½ (41½, 45½, 47½)"
Length: 24 (24½, 25, 25½)"
Sleeve width at underarm: 17¼ (18¼, 19¼, 20¼)"

MATERIALS

Lion Brand's *Wool-Ease* (worsted weight, 80% acrylic/20% wool; 3 oz; approx 197 yds), 3 (4, 5, 6) skeins Terra Cotta #134 (A), 1 (1, 1, 2) skeins Copper #190 (B), 3 (4, 5, 5) skeins Loden #177 (C), and 3 (3, 3, 4) skeins Espresso #128 (D)
Crochet hooks, sizes G/6 and H/8 or size needed to obtain gauge

GAUGE

In Mélange Patt, with larger hook, 16 sts and 19 rows = 4".
To measure your gauge, make a test swatch as follows: With larger hook and A, ch 20.
Work Mélange Patt for nineteen rows total. Fasten off.
Piece should measure 4¾" wide and 4" long. **To save time, take time to check gauge.**

NOTES

Picot sc = Insert hook into next st, yarn over and pull up a loop, (yarn over and draw it through one loop on hook) three times, yarn over and draw it through two loops on hook.
To decrease, work a dec sc to combine the first 2 sts and/or the last 2 sts of the row.
Dec sc = (Insert hook into next st and pull up a loop) twice, yarn over and draw it through all three loops on hook.
To increase, work 2 sts into one st.
To change color, work until 2 loops rem on hook; with the new color, complete the st; fasten off the old color.

SIDEWAYS RIB PATT

(Over any number of ch)
Foundation Row: Sc into second ch from hook and into each ch across. Ch 1, turn.
Patt Row: Sc into the back loop of each sc across. Ch 1, turn.
Repeat Patt Row.

MÉLANGE PATT

(Ch mult. of 4)
Foundation Row (RS): Sc into second ch from hook and into each ch across. Ch 1, turn.
Row 1 (WS): With A, sc into each sc across. Ch 1, turn.
Row 2: With A, sc into each sc across. Change to B, ch 1, turn.

Row 3: With B, *sc into first sc, picot sc into next sc. Repeat from * across, ending row with sc into last sc. Change to C, ch 1, turn.
Rows 4 and 5: With C, sc into each st across. When Row 5 is completed, change to D, ch 1, turn.
Rows 6 and 7: With D, sc into each sc across. When Row 7 is completed, change to C, ch 1, turn.
Row 8: With C, sc into first sc, *FPDC into next sc three rows below, skip sc behind the FPDC just made, sc into next 3 sc. Repeat from * across, ending row with FPDC into next sc three rows below, skip sc behind the FPDC just made, sc into last sc. Ch 1, turn.
Row 9: With C, sc into each st across. Change to A, ch 1, turn.
Rows 10 and 11: With A, sc into each sc across. When Row 11 is completed, change to B, ch 1, turn.
Rows 12-14: With B, sc into each sc across. When Row 14 is completed, change to C, ch 1, turn.
Row 15: With C, work same as Row 3. Change to D, ch 1, turn.
Rows 16 and 17: With D, sc into each sc across. When Row 17 is completed, change to A, ch 1, turn.
Rows 18 and 19: With A, sc into each sc across. When Row 19 is completed, change to D, ch 1, turn.
Row 20: With D, work same as Row 8. Ch 1, turn.

Row 21: With D, sc into each st across. Change to C, ch 1, turn.

Rows 22 and 23: With C, sc into each st across. When Row 23 is completed, change to A, ch 1, turn.

Row 24: With A, sc into each sc across. Ch 1, turn.

Repeat Rows 1-24 for patt.

BACK

With larger hook and A, ch 80 (84, 92, 96). Beg Mélange Patt, and cont even on 79 (83, 91, 95) sts until piece measures approx 23 (23^1/$_2$, 24, 24^1/$_2$)" from beg, ending after WS row. Ch 1, turn.

Shape Neck: Next Row (RS): Work patt as established across first 28 (30, 33, 35) sts, ch 1, turn, leaving rest of row unworked. Dec 1 st at neck edge every row twice—26 (28, 31, 33) sts rem. Cont even until piece measures approx 24 (24^1/$_2$, 25, 25^1/$_2$)" from beg. Fasten off.

For second side of neck, with RS facing, skip the middle 23 (23, 25, 25) sts, attach yarn with a slip st to next st and ch 1. Cont in patt as established to end row. Complete as for first side.

FRONT

Work as for back until piece measures approx 21^1/$_2$ (22, 22^1/$_2$, 23)" from beg, ending after WS row.

Shape Neck: Next Row (RS): Work patt as established across first 33 (35, 38, 40) sts, ch 1, turn, leaving rest of row unworked. Dec 1 st at neck edge every row seven times—26 (28, 31, 33) sts rem. Cont even until piece measures approx 24 (24^1/$_2$, 25, 25^1/$_2$)" from beg. Fasten off.

For second side of neck, with RS facing, skip the middle 13 (13, 15, 15) sts, attach yarn with a slip st to next st and ch 1. Cont in patt as established to end row. Complete as for first side.

SLEEVES

With larger hook and A, ch 36 (36, 40, 40).

Beg Mélange Patt, and inc 1 st each side every other row 0 (4, 4, 7) times, then every fourth row 17 (15, 15, 14) times—69 (73, 77, 81) sts. Cont even until sleeve measures approx 17^3/$_4$ (18, 18, 18^1/$_2$)" from beg. Fasten off.

FINISHING

Sew shoulder seams.

Neckband: With RS facing and smaller hook, attach A with a slip st to neck edge of right shoulder seam and ch 1. Work 65 (65, 71, 71) sc around neckline. Join with a slip st to first sc. Fasten off.

With smaller hook and A, ch 15. Work Sideways Rib Patt until piece, when slightly stretched, fits around neckline—14 sc each row. Fasten off. Sew foundation row of neckband to the last row of the neckband. Sewing through back loops of each sc, sew neck ribbing into place in neckline, placing seam at center of back neck.

Place markers 8^1/$_2$ (9, 9^1/$_2$, 10)" down from shoulders. Set in sleeves between markers. Sew sleeve and side seams.

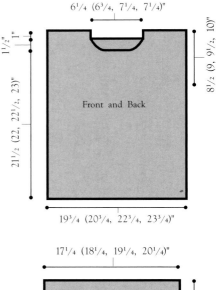

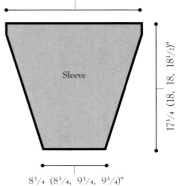

Child's Basketweave Cardigan

ADVANCED SKILL LEVEL

SIZES
Child's size 8 (10, 12, 14). Instructions are for smallest size, with changes for other sizes noted in parentheses as necessary.

FINISHED MEASUREMENTS
Chest (Buttoned): 35$\frac{1}{2}$ (36$\frac{1}{2}$, 39$\frac{1}{2}$, 40$\frac{1}{2}$)"
Length: 19$\frac{1}{2}$ (20$\frac{1}{2}$, 21$\frac{1}{2}$, 22$\frac{1}{2}$)"
Sleeve width at underarm: 15 (16, 16, 17)"

MATERIALS
Coats and Clark's *TLC* (heavy worsted weight, 100% acrylic; 5 oz; approx 253 yds), 8 (9, 9, 10) skeins Amber #5644
Crochet hooks, sizes H/8 and I/9 or size needed to obtain gauge
Six 1" buttons (JHB International's *Autumn Leaf Style #80013* was used on sample garment)

GAUGE
In Basketweave Patt, with larger hook, 16 sts and 11 rows = 4".
To measure your gauge, make a test swatch as follows: With larger hook, ch 24.
Foundation Row: Dc into fourth ch from hook and into each ch across—22 dc total. Ch 2, turn.
Next Row: Skip first st, *FPDC into next 4 sts, BPDC into next 4 sts. Repeat from * across, ending row with FPDC into next 4 sts, hdc into top of turning-ch. Ch 2, turn.

Repeat last row nine *more* times.
Fasten off.
Piece should measure 5$\frac{1}{2}$" wide and 4" long. **To save time, take time to check gauge.**

NOTES
To decrease, work a dec hdc to combine the first 2 sts and/or the last 2 sts of the row.
Dec hdc = (Yarn over, insert hook into next st and pull up a loop) twice, yarn over and draw it through all five loops on hook.
Dec sc = (Insert hook into next st and pull up a loop) twice, yarn over and draw it through all three loops on hook.
To increase, work 2 sts into one st.
Each dc, FPDC, BPDC, hdc, turning-ch-3, and turning-ch-2 counts as one st.

RIB PATT
(Over an even number of ch)
Foundation Row (RS): Dc into fourth ch from hook and into each ch across. Ch 2, turn.
Row 1 (WS): Skip first st, *FPDC into next st, BPDC into next st. Repeat from * across, ending row with hdc into top of turning-ch. Ch 2, turn.
Row 2: Skip first st, *FPDC into next st, BPDC into next st. Repeat from * across, ending row with hdc into top of turning-ch-2. Ch 2, turn.
Repeat Rows 1 and 2 for patt.

VERSION A OF BASKETWEAVE PATT
(Over a multiple of 8 + 6 sts)
Foundation Row (RS): Dc into fourth ch from hook and into each ch across. Ch 2, turn.
Patt Row: Skip first st, *FPDC into next 4 sts, BPDC into next 4 sts. Repeat from * across, ending row with FPDC into next 4 sts, hdc into top of turning-ch. Ch 2, turn.
Repeat Patt Row.

VERSION B OF BASKETWEAVE PATT
(Over a multiple of 8 + 2 sts)
Foundation Row (RS): Dc into fourth ch from hook and into each ch across. Ch 2, turn.
Patt Row 1: Skip first st, *FPDC into next 4 sts, BPDC into next 4 sts. Repeat from * across, ending row with hdc into top of turning-ch. Ch 2, turn.
Patt Row 2: Skip first st, *BPDC into next 4 sts, FPDC into next 4 sts. Repeat from * across, ending row with hdc into top of turning-ch-2. Ch 2, turn.
Repeat Patt Rows 1 and 2 for patt.

BACK
With smaller hook, ch 72 (76, 80, 84). Beg Rib Patt, and work even on 70 (74, 78, 82) sts until piece measures approx 1$\frac{1}{2}$" from beg, ending after WS row. Change to larger hook, ch 2, turn.

Beg Version A (B, A, B) of Basketweave Patt, and work even until piece measures approx 18$\frac{1}{2}$ (19$\frac{1}{2}$, 20$\frac{1}{2}$, 21$\frac{1}{2}$)" from beg, ending after WS row. Ch 2, turn.

Shape Neck: Next Row (RS): Cont patt as established, work across first 22 (24, 26, 28) sts, ch 2, turn, leaving rest of row unworked. Cont even in patt as established on this side until piece measures 19¹/₂ (20¹/₂, 21¹/₂, 22¹/₂)" from beg. Fasten off.

For second side of neck, with RS facing, skip the middle 26 sts, attach yarn with a slip st to next st and ch 2. Cont in patt as established to end row. Complete same as first side.

LEFT FRONT
With smaller hook, ch 36 (36, 40, 40). Beg Rib Patt, and work even on 34 (34, 38, 38) sts until piece measures approx 1¹/₂" from beg, ending after WS row. Change to larger hook, ch 2, turn.

Beg Version B (B, A, A) of Basketweave Patt, and work even until piece measures approx 12¹/₂ (13¹/₂, 14¹/₂, 15¹/₂)" from beg, ending after RS row. Ch 2, turn.

Shape Neck: Cont in patt and dec 1 st at neck edge every row 8 (4, 8, 4) times, then every other row 4 (6, 4, 6) times—22 (24, 26, 28) sts rem. Cont even until piece measures same as back. Fasten off.

RIGHT FRONT
Work same as left front, *except* reverse all shaping.

SLEEVES
With smaller hook, ch 32 (32, 36, 36). Beg Rib Patt, and work even on 30 (30, 34, 34) sts until piece measures approx 1¹/₂" from beg, ending after WS row. Change to larger hook, ch 2, turn.

Beg Version A (A, B, B) of Basketweave Patt, and inc 1 st each side every other row 15 (17, 11, 13) times, then every fourth row 0 (0, 4, 4) times—60 (64, 64, 68) sts—working new sts into Basketweave Patt. Cont even until piece measures approx 13³/₄ (15¹/₄, 16¹/₄, 17³/₄)" from beg. Fasten off.

FINISHING
Sew shoulder seams.

Front Bands: Row 1: With RS facing and smaller hook, attach yarn with a slip st to lower right front edge and ch 1. Work 175 (183, 191, 199) sc along right front edge, around back of neck, and down left front edge. Ch 1, turn.

Next Row: Work sc into each sc, working 2 sc into each sc at beg of front neck shaping on both sides and working a dec sc at beg of both sides of back neck shaping.

Repeat last row until band measures approx ¹/₂" from beg. Place markers along right front edge for girl's cardigan and along left front edge for boy's cardigan for six evenly-spaced buttonholes, making the first and last ¹/₄" from beg of front neck shaping and lower edge.

Buttonhole Row: Cont in sc as before, and make six buttonholes where marked by working (ch 3, skip next 3 sc).

Next Row: Cont in sc as before, working 3 sc into each ch-3 sp of previous row.

Cont in sc as established until front bands measure approx 1" from beg. Fasten off.

Place markers 7¹/₂ (8, 8, 8¹/₂)" down from shoulders. Set in sleeves between markers. Sew sleeve and side seams. Sew on buttons.

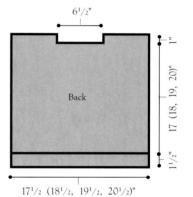

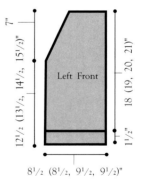

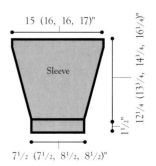

holiday jewels

Take the chill out of winter
with these richly-colored basics. Multi-colored
and tweedy yarns add flair without any extra effort.

Man's Houndstooth Pullover

INTERMEDIATE SKILL LEVEL

SIZES

Man's Small (Medium, Large, Extra-Large). Instructions are for smallest size, with changes for other sizes noted in parentheses as necessary.

FINISHED MEASUREMENTS

Chest: 42$^1/_2$ (46$^1/_2$, 50$^1/_2$, 54$^1/_2$)"
Length: 26 (27, 27$^1/_2$, 28)"
Sleeve width at underarm: 19$^1/_4$ (20$^1/_4$, 21$^1/_4$, 22$^1/_4$)"

MATERIALS

Lion Brand's *Wool-Ease* (worsted weight, 86% acrylic/10% wool/4% rayon; 3 oz; approx 197 yds), 7 (7, 8, 9) skeins Hunter Green Sprinkles #131 (A) and 4 (5, 6, 7) skeins Navy Sprinkles #110 (B)
Crochet hooks, sizes G/6 and H/8 or size needed to obtain gauge

GAUGE

With larger hook, in Houndstooth Patt, 16 hdc and 11 rows = 4".
To measure your gauge, make a test swatch as follows: With larger hook and A, ch 17.
Foundation Row: Hdc into third ch from hook and into each ch across—16 hdc total. Ch 2, turn.
Row 1: Skip first hdc, hdc into each st across, ending row with hdc into top of turning-ch-2. Ch 2, turn.
Repeat last row nine *more* times. Fasten off.
Piece should measure 4" square. **To save time, take time to check gauge.**

NOTES

To decrease, work a dec hdc to combine the first 2 sts and/or the last 2 sts of the row.
Dec hdc = (Yarn over, insert hook into next st and pull up a loop) twice, yarn over and draw it through all five loops on hook.
To increase, work 2 sts into one st.
To change color, work until 3 loops rem on hook; with the new color, complete the st; fasten off the old color. Each FPDC, BPDC, hdc, and turning-ch-2 counts as one st.

RIB PATT

(Over an odd number of ch)
Foundation Row (RS): Dc into fourth ch from hook and into each ch across. Ch 2, turn.
Row 1 (WS): Skip first st, *FPDC into next st, BPDC into next st. Repeat from * across, ending row with FPDC into next st, hdc into top of turning-ch. Ch 2, turn.
Row 2: Skip first hdc, *BPDC into next st, FPDC into next st. Repeat from * across, ending row with BPDC into next st, hdc into top of turning-ch-2. Ch 2, turn.
Repeat Rows 1 and 2 for patt.

HOUNDSTOOTH PATT

(Mult. 4 + 1 sts)
See chart, page 85.

BACK

With smaller hook and A, ch 87 (95, 103, 111). Work Rib Patt until piece measures approx 2$^1/_2$" from beg, ending after WS row—85 (93, 101, 109) sts each row. Ch 2, turn.

Change to larger hook, beg Houndstooth Patt in hdc and work even until piece measures approx 25 (26, 26$^1/_2$, 27)" from beg, ending after WS row. Ch 2, turn.

Shape Neck: Next Row (RS): Work in patt as established across first 28 (32, 36, 40) sts. Ch 2, turn, leaving rest of row unworked.

Dec 1 st at neck edge at beg of next row, then cont even on 27 (31, 35, 39) sts until this side measures approx 26 (27, 27$^1/_2$, 28)" from beg. Fasten off.

For second side of neck, with RS facing, skip the middle 29 sts, attach yarn with a slip st to next st and ch 2. Complete as for first side.

FRONT

Work as for back until piece measures approx 23 (24, 24$^1/_2$, 25)" from beg, ending after WS row. Ch 2, turn.

Shape Neck: Next Row (RS): Work in patt as established across first 33 (37, 41, 45) sts. Ch 2, turn, leaving rest of row unworked.

Dec 1 st at neck edge every row six times—27 (31, 35, 39) sts rem.

Cont even until this side measures the same as back to shoulders. Fasten off.

For second side of neck, with RS facing, skip the middle 19 sts, attach yarn with a slip st to next st and ch 2. Complete as for first side.

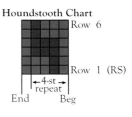

Houndstooth Chart

Row 6

Row 1 (RS)

←4-st→
repeat

End   Beg

Key: ■ = A
■ = B

Note: Each square represents
one hdc or turning-ch-2.

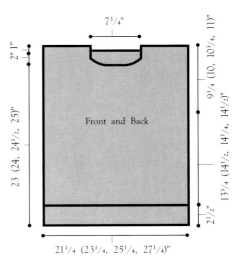

7³/₄"

2"1"

9³/₄ (10, 10³/₄, 11)"

Front and Back

13³/₄ (14¹/₂, 14¹/₄, 14¹/₂)"

23 (24, 24¹/₂, 25)"

2¹/₂"

21¹/₄ (23¹/₄, 25¹/₄, 27¹/₄)"

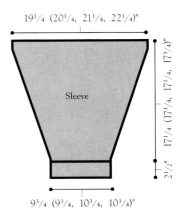

19¹/₄ (20¹/₄, 21¹/₄, 22¹/₄)"

17¹/₄ (17¹/₄, 17¹/₄, 17³/₄)"

Sleeve

2¹/₂"

9³/₄ (9³/₄, 10³/₄, 10³/₄)"

SLEEVES

With smaller hook and A, ch 41 (41, 45, 45). Work Rib Patt until piece measures approx 2¹/₂" from beg, ending after WS row—39 (39, 43, 43) sts each row. Ch 2, turn.

Change to larger hook, beg Houndstooth Patt in hdc, and inc 1 st each side every other row 16 (20, 20, 23) times, then every fourth row 3 (1, 1, 0) times—77 (81, 85, 89) sts.

Cont even until piece measures approx 19³/₄ (19³/₄, 19³/₄, 20¹/₄)" from beg. Fasten off.

FINISHING

Sew shoulder seams.

Neckband: With RS facing, smaller hook, and A, attach yarn with a slip st to neck edge of right shoulder seam and ch 3.

Rnd 1: Work 89 dc evenly around neckline. Join with a slip st to top of ch-3. Ch 2, do not turn.

Rnd 2: Skip first st, *FPDC into next st, BPDC into next st. Repeat from * around, ending rnd with FPDC, slip st to top of ch-2. Ch 2.

Repeat Rnd 2 until band measures approx 1" from beg. Fasten off.

Place markers 9³/₄ (10, 10³/₄, 11)" down from shoulders. Set in sleeves between markers.

Sew sleeve and side seams.

Woman's Chenille Vest

INTERMEDIATE SKILL LEVEL

SIZES

Woman's Small (Medium, Large, Extra-Large). Instructions are for smallest size, with changes for other sizes noted in parentheses as necessary.

FINISHED MEASUREMENTS

Bust (Buttoned): 34 (39, 43^3/$_4$, 48^3/$_4$)" Length (Excluding Edging): 24 (25, 25^1/$_2$, 26)"

MATERIALS

Lion Brand's *Chenille Sensations* (heavy worsted weight, 100% Acrylan® acrylic; 1^2/$_5$ oz; approx. 87 yds), 10 (11, 12, 13) skeins Amsterdam Print #409
Crochet hook, sizes G/6 and H/8 or size needed to obtain gauge
One 1" button (JHB International's *Tortola Style #71983* was used on sample garment)

GAUGE

With larger hook, in Lace Patt, 25 sts and 10 rows = 5" wide and 4" long. To measure your gauge, make a test swatch as follows: With larger hook, ch 26.
Work ten rows of Lace Patt.
Fasten off.
Piece should measure 5" wide and 4" long. **To save time, take time to check gauge.**

NOTES

In Lace Patt, each sc, dc, and ch counts as one st; each turning-ch-5 counts as three sts.
Dec sc = (Insert hook into next st and pull up a loop) twice, yarn over and draw it through all three loops on hook.

LACE PATT

(Ch mult. 6 + 2)
Foundation Row (RS): Sc into second ch from hook, *skip next 2 ch, 5 dc into next ch, skip next 2 ch, sc into next ch. Repeat from * across. Ch 5, turn.
Row 1 (WS): Skip first sc and next 2 dc, *sc into next dc, ch 2, skip next 2 dc, dc into next sc, ch 2, skip next 2 dc. Repeat from * across, ending row with sc into next dc, ch 2, skip next 2 dc, dc into last sc. Ch 1, turn.
Row 2: Sc into first dc, *skip next ch-2 sp, 5 dc into next sc, skip next ch-2 sp, sc into next dc. Repeat from * across, ending row with skip next ch-2 sp, 5 dc into next sc, sc into third ch of turning-ch-5. Ch 5, turn.
Repeat Rows 1 and 2 for patt.

BACK

With larger hook, ch 86 (98, 110, 122). Beg Lace Patt, and work even on 85 (97, 109, 121) sts until piece measures approx 15 (15^1/$_2$, 16, 16)" from beg, ending after WS row. *Do not ch 1 to turn.*

Shape Armholes: Next Row (RS): Slip st into first 13 (19, 19, 25) sts, ch 1, sc into same st as slip st, *skip next ch-2 sp, 5 dc into next sc, skip next ch-2 sp, sc into next dc. Repeat from * across, leaving last 12 (18, 18, 24) sts unworked—61 (61, 73, 73) sts. Ch 5, turn.

Cont even in Lace Patt until piece measures approx 23^1/$_4$ (24^1/$_4$, 24^3/$_4$, 25^1/$_4$)" from beg, ending after WS row. Ch 1, turn.

Shape Neck: Next Row (RS): Work patt as established across first 13 (13, 19, 19) sts, ch 5, turn, leaving rest of row unworked.

Cont one row even in patt as established on this side. Fasten off.

For second side of neck, with RS facing, skip the middle 35 sts, attach yarn with a slip st to next st and ch 1. Sc into same st as slip st, *skip next ch-2 sp, 5 dc into next sc, skip next ch-2 sp, sc into next dc. Repeat from * across, ending row with skip next ch-2 sp, 5 dc into next sc, sc into third ch of turning-ch-5. Ch 5, turn. Complete as for first side.

LEFT FRONT

With larger hook, ch 44 (50, 56, 62). Beg Lace Patt, and work even on 43 (49, 55, 61) sts until piece measures approx 15 (15^1/$_2$, 16, 16)" from beg, ending after WS row. *Do not ch 1 to turn.*

Shape Armhole: Next Row (RS): Slip st into first 13 (19, 19, 25) sts, ch 1, sc into same st as slip st, *skip next ch-2 sp, 5 dc into next sc, skip next ch-2 sp, sc into next dc. Repeat from * across, ending row with skip next ch-2 sp, 5 dc into next sc, sc into third ch of turning-ch-5. Ch 5, turn.

Cont even in Lace Patt on 31 (31, 37, 37) sts until piece measures approx 20^1/$_2$ (21^1/$_2$, 22, 22^1/$_2$)" from beg, ending after WS row.

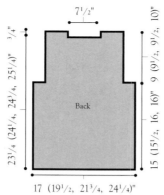

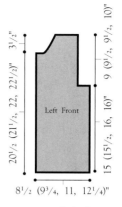

Shape Neck: Decrease Row 1 (RS): Cont in patt as established until 12 sts rem in row, ending row with skip next ch-2 sp, 3 dc into next sc, skip next ch-2 sp, dc into next dc. Ch 1, turn, leaving rest of row unworked.

Dec Row 2: Skip first dc, *sc into next dc, ch 2, skip next 2 dc, dc into next sc, ch 2, skip next 2 dc. Repeat from * across, ending row with sc into next dc, ch 2, dc into last sc. Ch 1, turn.

Dec Row 3: Cont patt as established until 6 sts rem in row, ending row with skip next ch-2 sp, sc into next dc, skip next ch-2 sp, dc into last sc. *Do not ch to turn.*

Dec Row 4: Skip first dc, skip next sc, skip next 2 dc, slip st into next dc, ch 1, sc into same place as last slip st, ch 2, skip next 2 dc, dc into next sc, *ch 2, skip next 2 dc, sc into next dc, ch 2, skip next 2 dc, dc into next sc. Repeat from * across. Ch 1, turn.

Dec Row 5: Same as Row 2 of Lace Patt, ending row with skip next last ch-2 and sc—13 (13, 19, 19) sts rem. Ch 5, turn.

Cont even in patt as established until piece measures the same as back. Fasten off.

RIGHT FRONT

Complete same as for left front until piece measures approx 15 (15½, 16, 16)" from beg, ending after WS row. *Do not ch 5 to turn.*

Shape Armhole: Next Row (RS): Cont in patt as established until 12 (18, 18, 24) sts rem in row. Ch 1, turn, leaving rest of row unworked.

Cont even in Lace Patt until piece measures approx 20½ (21½, 22, 22½)" from beg, ending after WS row. *Do not ch 1 to turn.*

Shape Neck: Dec Row 1 (RS): Slip st into first 7 sts, ch 3, skip first dc and next ch-2 sp, 3 dc into next sc, *skip next ch-2 sp, sc into next dc, skip next ch-2 sp, 5 dc into next sc. Repeat from * across, ending row with skip next ch-2 sp, sc into third ch of turning-ch-5. Ch 5, turn.

Dec Row 2: Skip first sc and next 2 dc, *sc into next dc, ch 2, skip next 2 dc, dc into next sc, ch 2, skip next 2 dc. Repeat from * across, ending row with sc into next dc. Ch 3, turn, leaving rest of row unworked.

Dec Row 3: Skip first sc and next ch-2 sp, *sc into next dc, skip next ch-2 sp, 5 dc into next sc, skip next ch-2 sp. Repeat from * across, ending row with sc into next dc, skip next ch-2 sp, 5 dc into next sc, sc into third ch of turning-ch-5. Ch 5, turn.

Dec Row 4: Skip first sc and next 2 dc, *sc into next dc, ch 2, skip next 2 dc, dc into next sc, ch 2, skip next 2 dc. Repeat from * across, ending row with sc into next dc. Ch 3, turn, leaving rest of row unworked.

Dec Row 5: Same as Dec Row 3—13 (13, 19, 19) sts rem.

Complete same as left front.

FINISHING

Lower Back Edging: With RS facing and smaller hook, attach yarn with a slip st to first sc and ch 1.

Row 1 (RS): Working along opposite side of foundation ch, sc into same st as slip st, *skip next 2 ch, 5 dc into next ch, skip next 2 ch, sc into next ch. Repeat from * across. Fasten off.

Front Lower Borders: With RS facing and smaller hook, attach yarn with a slip st to first sc and ch 1. Complete same as back lower edging.

Sew shoulder seams. Sew side seams.

Front Bands: With RS facing and smaller hook, attach yarn with a slip st to lower right front edge and ch 1. Work two rows of sc along right front edge, around neckline, and down left front edge, working 2 sc at beg of each front neck shaping and working dec sc at beg of each back of neck shaping.

Next Row (RS): Work same as last row, working a ch-9 loop at beg of neck shaping on right front. Fasten off.

Armhole Edging: With RS facing and smaller hook, attach yarn with a slip st to center of underarm and ch 1. Work two rnds of sc around armhole, working a dec sc at top of side seam and at beg of armhole on both front and back. Fasten off.

Sew on button opposite buttonloop.

Baby's Tweed Cardigan

INTERMEDIATE SKILL LEVEL

SIZES
Infant's size 6 (12, 18) months. Instructions are for smallest size, with changes for other sizes noted in parentheses as necessary.

FINISHED MEASUREMENTS
Chest (Buttoned): 25 (26$\frac{1}{2}$, 29$\frac{1}{2}$)"
Length: 11 (12$\frac{1}{2}$, 13$\frac{1}{2}$)"
Sleeve width at underarm: 10 (10, 11)"

MATERIALS
Coats and Clark's *Red Heart Baby Soft* (light worsted weight, 64% acrylic/36% nylon; 6 oz; approx 478 yds), 2 (2, 3) skeins Light Teal Twinkle #8502
Crochet hooks, sizes F/5 and G/6 or size needed to obtain gauge
Five $\frac{5}{8}$" buttons (JHB International's *Anaheim Style #44848* was used on sample garment)

GAUGE
With larger hook, in Seed St Patt, 24 sts and 20 rows = 4".
To measure your gauge, make a test swatch as follows: With larger hook, ch 28.
Work Seed St Patt for twenty rows. Fasten off.
Piece should measure 4$\frac{1}{2}$" wide and 4" long. **To save time, take time to check gauge.**

NOTES
Each sc, hdc, ch-1 and ch-2 counts as one st.
Dec sc = (Insert hook into next st and pull up a loop) twice, yarn over and draw it through all three loops on hook.

RIB PATT
(Over an odd number of ch)
Foundation Row (RS): Dc into fourth ch from hook and into each ch across. Ch 2, turn.
Row 1 (WS): Skip first st, *FPDC into next st, BPDC into next st. Repeat from * across, ending row with FPDC into next st, hdc into top of turning-ch. Ch 2, turn.
Row 2: Skip first sc, *BPDC into next st, FPDC into next st. Repeat from * across, ending row with BPDC into next st, hdc into top of turning-ch-2. Ch 2, turn.
Repeat Rows 1 and 2 for patt.

SEED ST PATT
(Mult. 2 + 1 sts)
Foundation Row (RS): Sc into first st, *ch 1, skip next st, sc into next st. Repeat from * across. Ch 1, turn.
Row 1 (WS): Sc into first sc and ch-1 sp, *ch 1, skip next sc, sc into next ch-1 sp. Repeat from * across, ending row with sc into last sc. Ch 1, turn.
Row 2: Sc into first sc, *ch 1, skip next sc, sc into next ch-1 sp. Repeat from * across, ending row with ch 1, skip next sc, sc into last sc. Ch 1, turn.
Repeat Rows 1 and 2 for patt.

BACK
With smaller hook, ch 77 (83, 89). Work Rib Patt for four rows total—75 (81, 87) sts each row. Change to larger hook, ch 1, turn.

Next Row (RS): Work Foundation Row of Seed St Patt—75 (81, 87) sts. Ch 1, turn.

Cont even in Seed St Patt until piece measures approx 10 (11$\frac{1}{2}$, 12$\frac{1}{2}$)" from beg, ending after RS row.

Shape Neck: Next Row (WS): Cont patt as established across first 22 (24, 26) sts, ch 1, turn, leaving rest of row unworked.

Cont even on this side until piece measures approx 11 (12$\frac{1}{2}$, 13$\frac{1}{2}$)" from beg. Fasten off.

For second side of neck, with WS facing, skip the middle 31 (33, 35) sts, attach yarn with a slip st to next st and ch 1. Sc into same st as slip st, ch 1, sc into next ch-1 sp, work to end row. Complete as for first side.

LEFT FRONT
With smaller hook, ch 37 (39, 43). Work Rib Patt for four rows total—35 (37, 41) sts each row. Change to larger hook, ch 1, turn.

Next Row (RS): Work Foundation Row of Seed St Patt—35 (37, 41) sts. Ch 1, turn.

Cont even in Seed St Patt until piece measures approx 6 (7$\frac{1}{2}$, 8)" from beg, ending after RS row. Ch 1, turn.

Shape Neck: Next Row (WS): Dec sc to combine the first sc and ch-1 sp, *ch 1, skip next sc, sc into next ch-1 sp. Repeat from * across, ending row with sc into last sc. Ch 1, turn.

Next Row: Sc into first sc, *ch 1, skip next sc, sc into next ch-1 sp. Repeat from * across, ending row with ch 1, skip next sc, dec sc to combine next ch-1 sp and dec sc. Ch 1, turn.

Next Row: Dec sc to combine the first dec sc and ch-1 sp, *ch 1, skip next sc, sc into next ch-1 sp. Repeat from * across, ending row with sc into last sc. Ch 1, turn.

Repeat last two rows once (once, twice) *more*—30 (32, 34) sts rem.

Next Row (RS): Sc into first sc, *ch 1, skip next sc, sc into next ch-1 sp. Repeat from * across, ending row with sc into last st. Ch 1, turn.

Next Row: Dec sc to combine the first 2 sc, sc into next ch-1 sp, *ch 1, skip next sc, sc into next ch-1 sp. Repeat from * across, ending row with sc into last sc. Ch 1, turn.

Next Row: Sc into first sc, *ch 1, skip next sc, sc into next ch-1 sp. Repeat from * across, ending row with ch 1, skip next sc, sc into last st. Ch 1, turn.

Next Row: Dec sc to combine the first sc and ch-1 sp, *ch 1, skip next sc, sc into next ch-1 sp. Repeat from * across, ending row with sc into last sc. Ch 1, turn.

Repeat last four rows three *more* times— 22 (24, 26) sts rem. Cont even until piece measures the same as back to shoulders. Fasten off.

RIGHT FRONT

Work as for left front until piece measures approx 6 (7½, 8)" from beg, ending after RS row. Ch 1, turn.

Shape Neck: Next Row (WS): Work patt as established until 2 sts rem, ending row with dec sc to combine the last ch-1 sp and sc. Ch 1, turn.

Next Row: Dec sc to combine the dec sc and next ch-1 sp, *ch 1, skip next sc, sc into next ch-1 sp. Repeat from * across, ending row with ch 1, skip next sc, sc into last sc. Ch 1, turn.

Next Row: Work patt as established until 2 sts rem, ending row with dec sc to combine the last ch-1 sp and sc. Ch 1, turn.

Repeat last two rows once (once, twice) *more*—30 (32, 34) sts rem.

Next Row (RS): Sc into first sc and ch-1 sp, *ch 1, skip next sc, sc into next ch-1 sp. Repeat from * across. Ch 1, turn.

Next Row: Sc into first sc and ch-1 sp, *ch 1, skip next sc, sc into next ch-1 sp. Repeat from * across, ending row with dec sc to combine the last 2 sc. Ch 1, turn.

Next Row: Sc into first sc, *ch 1, skip next sc, sc into next ch-1 sp. Repeat from * across, ending row with ch 1, skip next sc, sc into last sc. Ch 1, turn.

Next Row: Sc into first sc and ch-1 sp, *ch 1, skip next sc, sc into next ch-1 sp. Repeat from * across, ending row with ch 1, skip next sc, dec sc to combine the next ch-1 sp and last sc. Ch 1, turn.

Repeat last four rows three *more* times— 22 (24, 26) sts rem. Cont even until piece measures the same as left front. Fasten off.

SLEEVES

With smaller hook, ch 41 (43, 47). Work Rib Patt for four rows total—39 (41, 45) sts each row. Change to larger hook, ch 1, turn.

Next Row (RS): Sc into first st, *ch 1, skip next st, sc into next st. Repeat from * across. Ch 1, turn.

For size six months only:
Inc Row 1: Sc into first sc, *ch 1, sc into next ch-1 sp, skip next sc. Repeat from * across, ending row with ch 1, sc into next ch-1 sp, ch 1, sc into last sc. Ch 1, turn.

Inc Row 2: Sc into first sc and ch-1 sp, *ch 1, skip next sc, sc into next ch-1 sp. Repeat from * across, ending row with sc into last sc. Ch 1, turn.

Inc Row 3: 2 Sc into first sc, *ch 1, skip next sc, sc into next ch-1 sp. Repeat from * across, ending row with ch 1, skip next sc, 2 sc into last sc. Ch 1, turn.

Inc Row 4: Sc into first sc, *ch 1, skip next sc, sc into next ch-1 sp. Repeat from * across, ending row with ch 1, skip next sc, sc into last sc. Ch 1, turn.

Repeat Inc Rows 1-4 four *more* times, then work Inc Row 1 once *more*—61 sts.

For sizes 12 and 18 months only:
Inc Row 1: Sc into first sc, *ch 1, sc into next ch-1 sp, skip next sc. Repeat from * across, ending row with ch 1, sc into next ch-1 sp, ch 1, sc into last sc. Ch 1, turn.

Inc Row 2: Sc into first sc and ch-1 sp, *ch 1, skip next sc, sc into next ch-1 sp. Repeat from * across, ending row with sc into last sc. Ch 1, turn.

Inc Row 3: Sc into first sc, *ch 1, skip next sc, sc into next ch-1 sp. Repeat from * across, ending row with ch 1, skip next sc, sc into last sc. Ch 1, turn.

Repeat Inc Rows 1-3 nine (ten) *more* times—61 (67) sts.

For all sizes:
Cont even on these 61 (61, 67) sts in Seed St Patt as established until piece measures approx 6 (7^{1}/$_{4}$, 8^{1}/$_{2}$)" from beg. Fasten off.

FINISHING
Sew shoulder seams.

Front Edges: With RS facing, attach yarn to lower right front edge and ch 1.

Row 1 (RS): Work sc evenly along right front edge, around neckline, and down left front edge. Ch 1, turn.

Work rows of sc, working 2 sc at beg of both front shapings and a dec sc at beg of both back neck shapings, until band measures approx ^{1}/$_{2}$" from beg. Place markers along right front edge for girl's cardigan and along left front edge for boy's cardigan for five evenly-spaced buttonholes, making the first and last ^{1}/$_{4}$" from lower edge and beg of neck shaping.

Buttonhole Row: Cont in sc as before, and make five buttonholes where marked by working (ch 2, skip next 2 sc).

Next Row: Cont in sc as before, working 2 sc into each ch-2 sp of previous row.

Cont in sc as established until band measures approx 1" from beg. Fasten off.

Place markers 5 (5, 5^{1}/$_{2}$)" down from shoulders. Set in sleeves between markers. Sew sleeve and side seams. Sew on buttons.

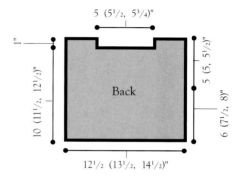

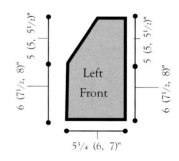

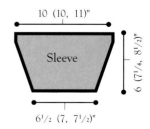

abbreviations

approx	approximately	FPTR	front post triple crochet	tog	together
beg	begin(ning)	hdc	half double crochet	tr	triple crochet
BPDC	back post double crochet	inc	increas(e)(ing)	WS	wrong side
BPTR	back post triple crochet	LH	left-hand	yds	yards
ch(s)	chain(s)	mult	multiple	YO	yarn over
ch-sp	chain space	oz	ounces	*	repeat instructions after
cont	continu(e)(ing)	patt(s)	pattern(s)		asterisk or between asterisks
dc	double crochet	rem	remain(ing)		across row or for as many
dec	decreas(e)(ing)	rnd(s)	round(s)		times as instructed
dtr	double triple crochet	RS	right side	( ) or [ ]	repeat enclosed instructions
FPSTS	front post stitches	sc	single crochet		for as many times as
FPDC	front post double crochet	sp(s)	space(s)		instructed or work all
FPDTR	front post double triple crochet	st(s)	stitch(es)		enclosed instructions in
					stitch or space indicated

CROCHET TERMINOLOGY

UNITED STATES		INTERNATIONAL
slip stitch (slip st)	=	single crochet (sc)
single crochet (sc)	=	double crochet (dc)
half double crochet (hdc)	=	half treble crochet (htr)
double crochet (dc)	=	treble crochet (tr)
triple crochet (tr)	=	double treble crochet (dtr)
double triple crochet (dtr)	=	triple treble crochet (ttr)
skip	=	miss

ALUMINUM CROCHET HOOKS

U.S.	B-1	C-2	D-3	E-4	F-5	G-6	H-8	I-9	J-10	K-10½	N	P	Q
Metric - mm	2.25	2.75	3.25	3.50	3.75	4.00	5.00	5.50	6.00	6.50	9.00	10.00	15.00

yarn choice and substitution

Each sweater in this book was designed for a specific yarn. Since many characteristics such as fiber content, texture, and twist can affect the way yarns appear and behave when crocheted, I recommend that you use the suggested yarn for each sweater.

If, however, you would like to substitute another yarn for your project, be sure to choose one of similar weight to the one called for in the materials section of the pattern. To determine the weight of the yarn you are working with, work up a swatch of solid single crochet at least 4" square. Count the number of stitches over 4" and refer to the table.

Yarn Weight	Stitches per 4"
Fingering weight	24 or more
Sport weight	22-24
Light worsted weight	20-22
Worsted weight	19-20
Heavy worsted weight	16-18
Bulky weight	15 or fewer

basic stitches and techniques

CHAIN

When beginning a first row of crochet in a chain, always skip the first chain from the hook and work into the second chain from hook (for single crochet), third ch from hook (for half double crochet), or fourth ch from hook (for double crochet), etc. (*Fig. 1*).

Fig. 1

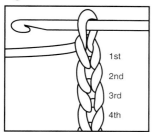

WORKING INTO THE CHAIN

Method 1: Insert hook into back ridge of each chain indicated (*Fig. 2a*).
Method 2: Insert hook under top two strands of each chain (*Fig. 2b*).

Fig. 2a

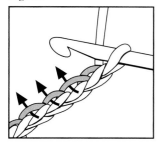

Fig. 2b

SLIP STITCH

(*abbreviated slip st*)
This stitch is used to attach new yarn, to join work, or to move the yarn across a group of stitches without adding height. Insert hook in stitch or space indicated, YO and draw through stitch and loop on hook (*Fig. 3*).

Fig. 3

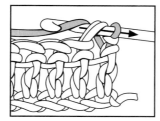

SINGLE CROCHET

(*abbreviated sc*)
Insert hook in stitch or space indicated, YO and pull up a loop, YO and draw through both loops on hook (*Fig. 4*).

Fig. 4

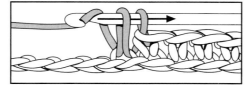

HALF DOUBLE CROCHET

(*abbreviated hdc*)
YO, insert hook in stitch or space indicated, YO and pull up a loop, YO and draw through all 3 loops on hook (*Fig. 5*).

Fig. 5

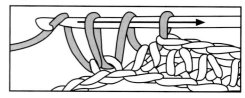

DOUBLE CROCHET

(*abbreviated dc*)
YO, insert hook in stitch or space indicated, YO and pull up a loop, YO and draw through 2 loops on hook (*Fig. 6a*), YO and draw through remaining 2 loops on hook (*Fig. 6b*).

Fig. 6a

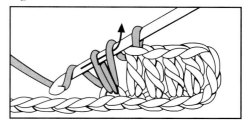

Fig. 6b

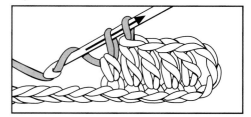

TRIPLE CROCHET
(abbreviated tr)

YO twice, insert hook in stitch or space indicated, YO and pull up a loop *(Fig. 7a)*, (YO and draw through 2 loops on hook) 3 times *(Fig. 7b)*.

Fig. 7a

Fig. 7b

FRONT POST DOUBLE CROCHET
(abbreviated FPDC)

YO, insert hook from **front** to **back** around post of stitch indicated, YO and pull up a loop *(Fig. 8)*, (YO and draw through 2 loops on hook) twice.

Fig. 8

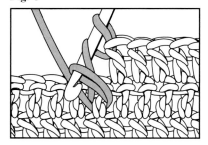

BACK POST DOUBLE CROCHET
(abbreviated BPDC)

YO, insert hook from **back** to **front** around post of stitch indicated, YO and pull up a loop *(Fig. 9)*, (YO and draw through 2 loops on hook) twice.

Fig. 9

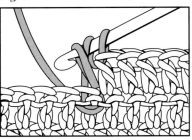

FRONT POST TRIPLE CROCHET
(abbreviated FPTR)

YO twice, insert hook from **front** to **back** around post of stitch indicated, YO and pull up a loop *(Fig. 10)*, (YO and draw through 2 loops on hook) 3 times.

Fig. 10

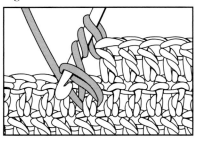

FRONT POST DOUBLE TRIPLE CROCHET
(abbreviated FPDTR)

YO 3 times, insert hook from **front** to **back** around post of stitch indicated, YO and pull up a loop *(Fig. 11)*, (YO and draw through 2 loops on hook) 4 times.

Fig. 11

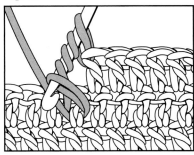

DECREASE SINGLE CROCHET

Pull up a loop in next 2 sts, YO and draw through all 3 loops on hook *(Fig. 12)* (**counts as one sc**).

Fig. 12

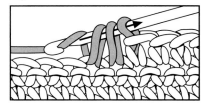

DECREASE HALF DOUBLE CROCHET

*YO, insert hook in **next** st, YO and pull up a loop; repeat from * once **more**, YO and draw through all 5 loops on hook *(Fig. 13)* (**counts as one hdc**).

Fig. 13

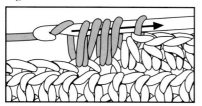

DECREASE DOUBLE CROCHET

*YO, insert hook in **next** st, YO and pull up a loop, YO and draw through 2 loops on hook; repeat from * once **more**, YO and draw through all 3 loops on hook *(Fig. 14)* (**counts as one dc**).

Fig. 14

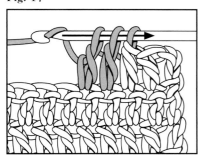

CHANGING COLOR

Work the last stitch to within one step of completion, hook new yarn *(Fig. 15a or 15b)* and draw through loops on hook. Cut old yarn and work over both ends unless otherwise specified.

Fig. 15a

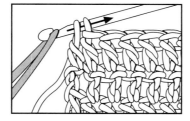

Fig. 15b

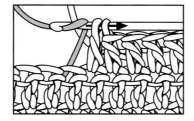

FRINGE

Cut a piece of cardboard 3" wide and $1/2$" longer than you want your finished fringe to be. Wind the yarn **loosely** and **evenly** around the cardboard until the card is filled, then cut across one end; repeat as needed.

Hold together half as many strands of yarn as desired for the finished fringe; fold in half. With **wrong** side facing and using a crochet hook, draw folded end up through a stitch or row and pull the loose ends through the folded end *(Figs. 16a & b)*; draw the knot up **tightly** *(Figs. 16c & d)*. Repeat, spacing as desired.

Lay flat on a hard surface and trim the ends.

Fig. 16a

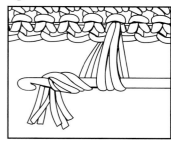

Fig. 16b

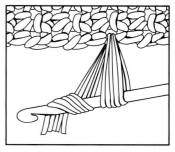

Fig. 16c

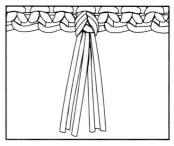

Fig. 16d

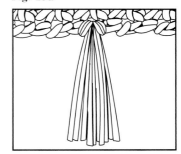

resources

THE CROCHET GUILD OF AMERICA:

To enjoy crochet camaraderie and to learn more about the craft, contact:
The Crochet Guild of America
2502 Lowell Road
Gastonia, NC 28054
(877) 852-9190
E-mail: cgoa@crochet.org
Website: www.crochet.org

MANUFACTURERS:

(These companies sell wholesale only. Contact them to locate retail stores in your area.)

Caron International
1481 West 2nd Street
P.O. Box 222
Washington, NC 27889
(800) 868-9194

Coats & Clark, Inc.
Consumer Service Dept.
P.O. Box 12229
Greenville, SC 29612-0229
www.coatsandclark.com

JHB International, Inc.
1955 South Quince Street
Denver, CO 80231
(303) 751-8100

Lily/Spinrite, Inc.
320 Livingstone Avenue South
Listowel, Ontario N4W 3H3 Canada
(519) 291-3780

Lion Brand Yarn
34 West 15th Street
New York, NY 10011
(212) 243-8995

MAIL ORDER SOURCES:

Annie's Attic
1 Annie Lane
Big Sandy, TX 75755
(800) 582-6643

Herrschner's and
Herrschner's Yarn Shoppe
2800 Hoover Road
Stevens Point, WI 54492
(800) 441-0838

Mary Maxim
2001 Holland Avenue
P.O. Box 5019
Port Huron, MI 48061
(800) 962-9504

INSTRUCTIONAL RESOURCES:

For additional technical information and creative inspiration, refer to one of the following books:

Aytes, Barbara. *Adventures in Crocheting.* Garden City, New York: Doubleday and Company, 1972.

Blackwell, Liz. *A Treasury of Crochet Patterns.* New York: Charles Scribner's Sons, 1971.

Duncan, Ida Riley. *The Complete Book of Needlecraft.* New York: Liveright, 1972.

Goldberg, Rhoda Ochser. *The New Crochet Dictionary.* New York: Crown, 1986.

Leapman, Melissa. *Crochet with Style.* Newtown, CT: Taunton Press, 2000.

Mariano, Linda. *The Encyclopedia of Knitting and Crochet Stitch Patterns.* New York: Van Nostrand Reinhold Company, 1976.

Matthews, Anne. *Vogue Dictionary of Crochet Stitches.* London: David and Charles, 1987.

Mountford, Debra, ed., *The Harmony Guide to Crocheting Techniques and Stitches.* New York: Harmony, 1992.

Righetti, Maggie. *Crocheting in Plain English.* New York: St. Martins Press, 1988.

Schapper, Linda P. *Complete Book of Crochet Stitch Designs.* New York: Sterling Publishing Company, 1985.

Threads editors. *Knitting Tips and Trade Secrets.* Newtown, CT: Taunton Press, 1996.

Westfall, Fran. *Encyclopedia of Knitting and Crochet Stitches.* New York: Bonanza Books, 1971.